HELLO $FIRSTNAME

PROFITING FROM PERSONALIZATION

RASMUS HOULIND   **FRANS RIEMERSMA**

ARILD HORSBERG   **MATTIAS ANDERSSON**

OMNICHANNEL
INSTITUTE

Paperback: 978-87-974428-0-7
Ebook: 978-87-974428-1-4
Audiobook: 978-87-974428-2-1

First paperback edition April 2023.

Edited by Hazel Bird
Cover art and Layout by Tobias Frost @ StudioFrost

Omnichannel Institute
Copenhagen, Denmark

OmnichannelInstitute.com

ADVANCE PRAISE

"Hello $FirstName is one of the best books on personalization I've read. Rasmus Houlind and his co-authors provide an excellent blueprint for implementing real-world personalization capabilities and developing the organizational capital to apply them effectively."

- SCOTT BRINKER, EDITOR, CHIEFMARTEC.COM

———

"It's continually important that we talk about personalization from a unified perspective and understanding. This book helps us achieve that common ground."

- FIONA SPOONER, MANAGING DIRECTOR, CONSUMER REVENUE, FINANCIAL TIMES

———

"Incredibly insightful views on personalization – the largest and most rapid ROI projects that our clients are implementing. Hello $FirstName is a must-read for B2C commerce in 2023."

- DOUG WEICH, CEO, SOPHELLE

———

"Personalization within marketing is extremely challenging but if done correctly, will become the key to your success. Hello $FirstName is by far one of the best books to help you navigate this complex universe and map out the crucial strategy needed. A must-have for every modern marketer!"

- FREDRIK SALZEDO, DIRECTOR, GLOBAL MARTECH AND AUTOMATIONS, HBO MAX AND DISCOVERY+

———

"Personalization might be all the rage right now but it's an amorphous beast that means different things to different brands. There is a real risk of derailing the movement towards more personalized customer experiences if we fail to define what it is, what it isn't, and what the common standards should be. I'd urge any customer-focused marketer to order Hello$FirstName today!"

- DAN BRAIN, CO-FOUNDER AND CONTENT DIRECTOR, MAD//FEST

———

"In the pursuit of a seamless customer experience and with today's digital possibilities, personalization has rightly become one of the most hyped marketing terms. This compact, coherent, and practice-oriented book not only offers novices a very good introduction to the topic, but certainly also inspires experts and helps organizations with common goal setting and efficient implementation through a comprehensible, uniform language. A definite reading recommendation."

- JESPER REISMANN, FORMER SVP OMNICHANNEL, HUGO BOSS

———

FOREWORD (1 OF 2)

Personalization. A conflicting, complex, seemingly endless topic that meanders between the great and the awful. The good and the evil. With everyone talking about it perpetually, and every year being the year of personalization, why do brands still struggle to make it work? For all the inherent belief in it as a marketing discipline and all the evidence that it works, there are very few publications out there about how to do it. Whatever it is. Until now.

This is exactly why I decided to write a book about personalization myself – *The Personalisation Paradox* (UK spelling, I know). Only to find that at exactly the same time, 1,000 km away, a very senior chief experience officer with a track record of more than 20 years, at one of the best marketing automation platforms in the world, Agillic, and already a twice-established author, was writing a book about personalization at exactly the same time. Personalization books are like buses; you wait around for ages for one and then two come along at the same time. It was game time.

It was important for Rasmus Houlind and his co-authors to add value by dispelling myths, providing evidence, and combining sources of material to enable genuine practical application. It wasn't the why or the what that was important, but the how. As practitioners, the 'how' is what we all need support in, and the dedication of Rasmus and his team, spending a whole year creating content for us all on our personalization journeys, is to be admired.

I instantly became green with envy at the much wittier book title, *Hello $FirstName*, and even more so at the desk research. On the back of their extensive first-hand experience with clients in the Nordics, Rasmus held numerous workshops with expert panels of practitioners, carried out countless interviews, and gained access to behind-the-scenes academic studies.

Having been with Rasmus throughout the journey, in which we have turned competition into friendship, I can honestly say after reading *Hello $FirstName* that it is unapologetically simple yet thorough. Arriving at a unified definition of personalization that takes into account all forms of marketing is no mean feat. I've changed my mind on multiple occasions from reading some of the content and evidence the book provides. The case studies are boutique yet relatable – and, ironically, personal.

Rasmus and his co-authors put all of this into practical applications that can be used by all, in both the Bowtie of Personalization and the Pyramid of Personalization. I feel this is the start of something really useful for brands. Their approach appreciates that personalization is part of a wider marketing belief system, not an insular siloed tactic on a website usually restricted to recommendations. To that end, this book really is unique in helping us to think about what personalization is and is not, and what it should be.

If, like all of us, you're struggling to personalize, or achieve another level in your personalization efforts, reading *Hello $FirstName* will give you much inspiration and practical conviction. And don't worry – you're not alone. Rasmus and his co-authors appreciate that this isn't easy. To that end, they provide enough context for your 30,000 ft view and enough detail for your 3 ft view. The result of which is a nice bow (tie) of supremely simple, a-ha moments of added value.

- David Mannheim, Author of 'The Personalisation Paradox'

FOREWORD (2 OF 2)

There is nothing more powerful than an idea whose time has come.

Bringing ideas to life is a thrilling and rewarding journey that requires passion, dedication, and perseverance. It's the process of turning dreams into tangible realities that can transform and improve our lives.

I met Rasmus Houlind, the primary author of this book, when I first took the helm of Agillic. My first encounter with this energized evangelist of personalization affected my way of dreaming, observing, understanding, analysing, and executing our business strategy and perhaps most importantly our way of defining our company purpose. I believe that personalization should rightfully be used to transform customers from anonymous consumers to valued individuals, creating a powerful bond between brands and their audiences. Yet, this is rarely a given and many brands never get there – even if they've invested heavily in the technology to support it.

When the idea of *Hello $FirstName* was born, I was thrilled to support Rasmus and his co-authors, Frans Riemersma, Arild Horsberg, and Mattias Andersson – all great movement leaders and co-dreamers from different countries. I realized that a profound treatment of personalization – what it is, what it isn't, and what it actually takes to succeed – would benefit everyone involved in marketing or even business today.

That's why I am delighted to introduce this book on the personalization movement. It is a comprehensive guide to understanding and implementing personalization strategies in marketing. The book covers both the fundamental principles and the mindset of working in personalization with real-life examples told by experts, many of them partners in our ecosystem. One of the strengths of this book is its ability to demystify the process and make it accessible to readers of all levels of expertise and from various marketing disciplines. Whether you are a business leader, marketer, or technologist or if you're working within advertising, marketing automation, or product recommendations, this book provides clear and actionable insights that can help you and your team to design, implement, and measure effective personalization strategies.

This book is also timely, given the rapidly evolving nature of technology and consumer behaviour. Rasmus and his co-authors have done a brilliant job of addressing these trends and providing practical advice for staying ahead of the curve.

Finally, I believe this book is essential reading for those concerned with future readiness in business. Personalization is not just a trend but a fundamental shift in how businesses engage with their customers. A transformational change.

I'm certain you'll enjoy reading this book as much as I have. It'll help you and your team work together with a host of new ideas and a new-found clarity about personalization. Use it to take personalized communication to new heights – heights we previously could only dream about.

- Emre Gürsoy, CEO of Agillic

CONTENTS

PART TWO
A PRACTITIONER'S VIEW ON PERSONALIZATION

PART THREE
THE PREREQUISITES FOR PERSONALIZATION

INTRODUCTION

The title of this book, *Hello $FirstName*, is a reference to what could very well be the most common example of personalization in the world: the salutation often used in an email or a LinkedIn connection request. In the article 'A History of Direct Marketing', Nat Ross traced the earliest use of personalized direct mail all the way back to 1870.[1] In 1940, marketers working for *Time* magazine discovered that personalized salutations increased response rates for direct mail by as much as six times.[2]

Although this effect has now largely worn off, most of us still regularly receive emails or direct mail with our first name copied in, either in the subject line of the email or at the beginning of the main part of the communication. Some will also have seen examples of this having gone wrong, where the letter or email actually says '$FirstName' – revealing some of the underlying logic of how communication is personalized.

However, as this book will show, there is much more to personalization than putting a person's first name into a subject line. So much more, in fact, that there is now considerable hype on the topic. Indeed, in his book, *The Personalisation Paradox* (2023), David Mannheim demonstrates how researchers, practitioners' associations, and technology providers have dubbed every single year between 2015 and 2022 'the year of personalization'![3]

Obviously, technology providers, agencies, and personalization professionals have a natural interest in keeping the hype alive to sell their services. If you take the promises of the average technology vendor at face value, personalization – and especially hyper-personalization at scale – is 'the new black' and more is always better. With the right technology – namely theirs – it will all be fun and easy and you will be able to deliver a hyper-personalized customer journey based on AI and predictive analytics to all customers in no time, and money will fall from the sky like sweet summer rain.

Amazon and Netflix are probably the two single most impressive cases regarding personalization, and over time they have been kind enough to share a lot about their processes and results.[4] But these cases don't stand alone, by any means. There is a whole array of positive cases to be inspired by.

However, the seasoned marketer knows that these successes don't create themselves! It takes hard work from a lot of people working together using the relevant technology (of which there is definitely no shortage). But successfully working together requires a common language and understanding, as well as clear goals. And with personalization being such a wide topic, this creates a lot of confusion, which leads to misunderstandings, and this in turn leads to personalization projects that are doomed to fail from the get-go, with all that entails in terms of broken promises, shattered careers, lost potential, and wasted money.

If you're a marketing practitioner, the worst case is that your CEO may have heard the term 'personalization' and believe you are already doing it because your company began the simple personalization of first names in its communication long ago. If this is the case, then you are unlikely to be getting the resources you need to take full advantage of personalization.

But how do marketers look at personalized communication among themselves? In sharp contrast to what is actually needed, many marketers seem comfortable with only a semi-clear definition of personalization and nevertheless happily use the term believing they understand its meaning and potential, and what it takes to achieve it.

The differences between how marketers understand personalization seem to be the greatest when marketers represent companies with different go-to-market models, which often correlate with different marketing practices. A person who is working in advertising for a large fast-moving consumer goods company will have a hard time finding common ground with a fellow marketer who is working in a born-digital direct-to-consumer company.

To add to the confusion, there has been a growing tendency towards 'personalization bashing' within marketing's own ranks since the late 2010s. For example, some marketers, especially within branding and advertising, have criticized the whole notion of doing personalization in the first place since it would never make sense and be way too expensive (in terms of labour costs) to produce one personalized version of a brand story for each customer.[5]

So, what is up and what is down? Is personalization – and more specifically hyper-personalization – a hoax? A freak of nature? A cross-breed between lazy marketers and greedy technology salespeople? Is it any wonder that the modern CEO struggles to understand the wonders of personalization when marketers disagree this much even among themselves?

This book is aimed at all marketers working with personalization, to help them get a clear understanding of the concept and share this with their team to ultimately create better results with the resources at hand. The first and second parts of the book focus on understanding the concept in detail and will be helpful for marketing practitioners of all levels. The last two parts focus on the prerequisites as well as the organizational foundation of personalization and will be particularly helpful to marketing leaders and CEOs wishing to guide their organization towards creating the best possible customer experience.

More precisely, this book's first goal (the focus of *Part I*) is to create a common definition of personalization that anyone within the field will be able to comprehend. Using this definition, you should be able not only to identify your own perspective on personalization but also to clearly see its shortcomings and what you are missing. This will allow you to fully grasp the concept and reap the potential benefits, or at least avoid unfortunate mis-investments.

To help us get closer to a common definition, we held dialogues with more than 90[6] people working within digital marketing and personalization around the world (see 'About the book'). These people helped us to define the problem and later the solution that you are now starting to read. We'd like to thank these people for feeling our pain, for giving us their perspectives again and again, and for participating in roundtable debates and interviews that helped us to get closer to a common perception and a model we can all use.

In *Part II*, we move on to consider the main model of this book. Through countless examples from companies across a variety of industries, we developed our main model for understanding personalization: the Bowtie of Personalization. In *Chapter 6*, we explain how the underlying parts constitute a model for personalization that brings clarity to the (m)admen of our time and the media buyers, the customer relationship management (CRM) managers, and the website and ecommerce managers alike. The practitioners we consulted found the metaphor strikingly helpful, but we also acknowledge its primarily masculine connotations. If you are more comfortable thinking of a bow, then please do so. The logic still applies.

Chapters 7, *8*, *10*, and *12* go deeper into the four corners of the Bowtie of Personalization: segments, messages, moments of truth, and content feeds. If you are new to personalization, this model will give you a detailed understanding of the topic. If you are already a skilled practitioner, you will most likely find the model both intuitive and easy to understand. Its purpose is to anchor your team conversations around personalization and help you to establish the optimal conditions for working together in this area. It will especially be useful for getting new team members on board and up to speed in terms of understanding personalization. The Bowtie of Personalization brings clarity to the 'what' of personalization.

The second goal of this book is to show what it is that makes personalization profitable in each of the major marketing disciplines. To do this, in chapters interspersed throughout *Part II*, we'll demonstrate how different parts of the model play the main role depending on the marketer's agenda: building campaigns (*Chapter 9*), automating marketing (*Chapter 11*), and meeting customers on inbound platforms such as websites and apps (*Chapter 13*). In other words, taking into account the specific use case and the medium, what should you as a marketer focus on to succeed with personalization? What are the levers you can pull in order to maximize profit in both the short term and the long term, and in which order should you pull them? The findings are summed up in a maturity model that we call the Pyramid of Personalization. This model explains the 'how' of personalization. More specifically, *Chapter 14* focuses on maturity within the personalized communication that the customers experience. In other words, it sums up three maturity levels for the *scope* of work that you produce to deliver personalized customer experiences. This is the front end of the pyramid.

On the back of a newly found nuanced view of the topic of personalization, *Part III* then explores the prerequisites for personalization, such as how well your core business performs, how well you've established brand awareness and brand trust, and how well you can access customer data. As a by-product of this exploration, we'll also consider who personalization is *not* for and hopefully honour the sceptics a little.

This part is especially meant for marketing leaders, who will inevitably face demands from senior management and employees alike. It serves as a reality check as to whether personalization is the right tactic for your business at all at this given time. Use it to fend off impatient senior management colleagues with unrealistic expectations or to get the funding you need to put the basics in place.

In *Part IV*, we'll explore what it takes to succeed with personalization from an organizational point of view. Answering these questions is the third goal of the book: How can skills, software, and governance go hand in hand to make personalization possible? And how can you manage this process sustainably with proper governance? The three main resources – skills, software, and governance – will be visualized across three maturity levels. These three levels constitute the back end of the Pyramid of Personalization.

This last part of the book is especially for you if you are a marketing leader with an omnichannel customer profit-and-loss responsibility and if personalization is well anchored among your senior management. It will give you guidance as to how you can manage personalization optimally at the macro level. Lastly in this part, we'll consider how to break through the glass ceilings that exist between the three maturity levels of the Pyramid of Personalization.

We do hope and believe you and your teams will find this book both helpful and entertaining.

THE AUTHORS' NOTE ON THE PROCESS

This book is not only a result of academic desk research. To make sure the concepts and models would be usable by real practitioners and strategists, approximately 90 people helped to evaluate the book's content and models. Countless interviews were held with experts from all over the world. Moreover, a series of six expert panels of practitioners from the Nordic capitals (Copenhagen, Oslo, and Stockholm) met to discuss, criticize, and suggest changes to the models and concepts and to supply their knowledge of case studies to learn from. Please refer to the chapter Acknowledgements in the back of this book for the full list of people who participated and helped this project come alive.

THE NORDIC NEED FOR EFFICIENCY IN PERSONALIZATION

It's no secret that the authors, the contributors, and the cases in this book have their centres of gravity firmly rooted in the Nordics. We realize this means that some of the examples may not be considered household brands by overseas audiences. With the modest population size of the Nordic countries, a rather large customer database often contains no more than 1–2 million customers. This means that all personalization efforts must be built with great efficiency in order to become profitable. The authors firmly believe that this need for efficiency, as well as the general digital maturity in the region, provides valuable lessons for all practitioners – especially those operating in larger markets, who should be able to leverage these lessons to reach unseen heights due to the sheer scale of their databases.

NOTES ON THE CASE STUDIES USED

To give the reader a feeling for how a practitioner thinks and which considerations go into creating a sustainable personalized customer experience, we've chosen to start most of the chapters in the book with case studies in the form of narratives. These narratives aren't meant to be 100% factual representations of past real-life situations. However, they are all rooted in the practice of the represented organizations and as such they *could* have happened as they are presented here. The people featured within the narratives are all real people and have participated in the creation of the narratives. We are aware that the supplemental case studies have a preponderance of companies using Agillic as their omnichannel marketing automation software. This is a natural consequence of the main author's affiliation and the popularity of this platform in the Nordics but has no impact on the theoretical points made or the potential results that can be obtained with this or any other comparable software.

ALL MODELS AND ILLUSTRATIONS ARE AVAILABLE AS DOWNLOADS

As a natural part of democratizing success with personalization and spreading the concepts and thoughts from this book to all practitioners, the authors encourage anyone interested in the topic to download the models and illustrations from the book on www.omnichannelinsti tute.com/resources.

PART ONE
WHAT IS PERSONALIZATION?

CHAPTER 1
THE HYPE OF PERSONALIZATION

For us, at least, the personalization hype started way back in 1993, when Don Peppers and Martha Rogers published *The One to One Future*.[1] Could we get to a place where all communication was individualized, or what is now called 'hyper-personalized', for each customer? A place where no one saw the same offers and messages? Surely that would be a good place where consumers would be happy and brands could make a lot of money?

Working in digital marketing before 2010 mostly meant building websites and ecommerce solutions. Advertising on Google was still fairly simple and direct marketing was mostly a matter of putting letters in envelopes. So, the fact that Peppers and Rogers envisioned a 'one-to-one future' as early as 1993 seems incredible.

In a personal conversation with one of the co-authors of *Make It All About Me*,[2] Colin Shearer, Peppers later shared how he and Rogers had thought of the book as a piece of 'mar-fi' – marketing fiction. At the time, they saw the one-to-one future as a very distant one – if it would ever be possible at all. Clearly, personalization was in its very infancy in 1993. Still, the thought stayed around.

CONSUMERS *EXPECT* PERSONALIZATION – AND BRANDS HAD BETTER DELIVER

Fast forward to McKinsey's *Next in Personalization 2021 Report*.[3] According to this study, 71% of consumers expect brands to deliver personalized interactions and 76% get frustrated when this doesn't happen. Does this mean that the one-to-one future is here, or at least that consumers believe it should be? Then we'd better get to work. In fact, a lot of marketers already are. We like to believe that the very soul of personalization – where the customer experience is tailored to each individual – is what appeals to many marketers due to it being more pleasant and presumably less annoying for the customer. But clearly there is a lot of money in personalization – for brands and tech companies alike.

The McKinsey report concludes that digitally native direct-to-consumer companies on average can attribute 25% of their revenue to personalized communication.[4] A 2022 study by Forrester Consulting, commissioned by Agillic, furthermore showed that so-called leaders in the field of personalization are twice as likely to see 10% or more annual growth in revenue.[5]

In our daily work, we constantly encounter companies and clients for whom personalization has made a significant difference. An example of this is the online fashion marketplace Miinto, which has seen its customer lifetime increase by as much as 31%.[6] In another example, the Danish health and beauty retailer Matas is using personalization and omnichannel marketing to increase the number of its omnichannel customers (customers shopping both online and offline). These customers are nearly worth twice as much as their single-channel peers.[7]

THE TECH HYPE OF PERSONALIZATION

Chief Martec is an American technology blog and research company headed by the world-famous Scott Brinker. Every year, Chief Martec puts together an overview of marketing technologies within multiple categories (see *Figure 1*).[8] This overview is called the Marketing Technology Landscape, and for 2022 the landscape was put together with help from the European company MartechTribe.[9] The growth in the number of named technology vendors in this landscape has been immense, from approximately 150 providers in 2011 to 9,932 providers in 2022. This is an increase of 6,521%. Obviously not all of these providers have solutions for personalization, but 17 of the 49 categories in the landscape are closely related to the topic.

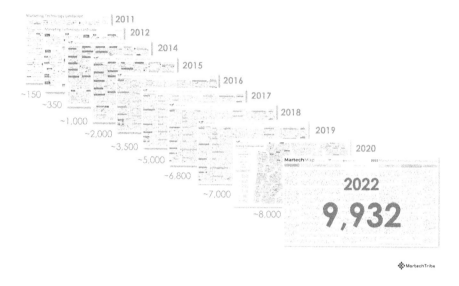

Figure 1. The Martech Landscape from 2011 to 2022, showing a growth of 6,521%

MartechTribe has also been looking more closely at which keywords (or even buzzwords) technology providers emphasize on their homepages. In 2022 they researched 226 marketing keywords sourced from Wikipedia and the global review platform G2 Crowd, and mapped them against 10,000 martech vendor websites (see *Figure 2*). Guess what – 'personalized marketing' was top of the list.[10]

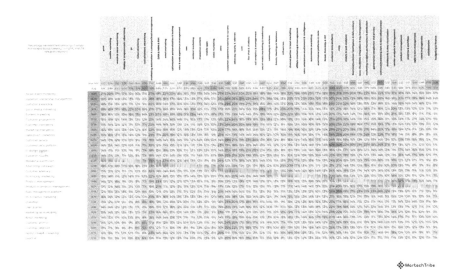

Figure 2. An overview of the most used marketing keywords across
10,000+ vendor websites: 'Personalized marketing' comes in at first
place. Source: MartechTribe.com

We're pretty sure most marketers would concur that these homepages
make it appear incredibly easy to get insanely good results by using
personalization.

HAS PERSONALIZATION TECHNOLOGY BECOME MATURE?

Gartner's 'hype cycles' illustrate how hyped versus mature a specific technology is in any given year.[11] Roughly speaking, a hype cycle consists of
five stages:

1. **Technology trigger** – commercial viability is unproven
2. **Peak of inflated expectations** – some companies take action but
   most don't
3. **Trough of disillusionment** – implementations fail to deliver
4. **Slope of enlightenment** – second- and third-generation products
   appear, and more enterprises fund pilots
5. **Plateau of productivity** – mainstream adoption starts to take off

For personalization technology, the developments over the years seem to indicate a growth in maturity.[12] If we look more closely at the entries called 'personalization', 'personalization engines', and 'multichannel marketing hubs', these all represent marketers' ability to implement personalization, and we should get a deeper insight into how Gartner perceives the progression. We have gathered these in *Figure 3*. First, multichannel marketing hubs, which are used mainly for outbound communication such as sending personalized emails and messages, have moved considerably along the hype cycle between 2018 and 2022, from the 'peak of inflated expectations' in 2018 far onto the 'plateau of productivity' in 2022. Second, 'personalization' had its very own entry which actually seemed to flourish from 2014, where it entered the hype cycle at the start of the 'trough of disillusionment' but quickly jumped into the 'slope of enlightenment' in the following year and then moved further up in 2016 and 2017. Then suddenly it disappeared. Instead we got 'personalization engines' appearing in the 'trough of disillusionment' in 2018. Moving slowly but steady forwards, in 2022 they were just about to enter the 'slope of enlightenment'. This raises a few questions. Was it a bad idea to put personalization into an engine? And what about the other categories called 'real-time marketing' and 'personification'? They also seem to relate to personalization. Either way – we can conclude two things. First, Gartner doesn't really seem to help us in terms of getting a clear understanding of the term 'personalization'. Second, the direction is clear: personalization is moving forward in terms of maturity.[13]

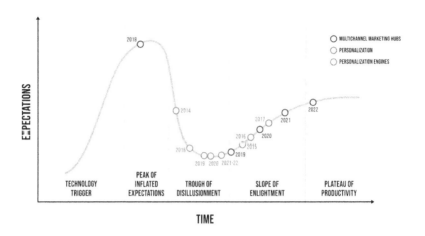

Figure 3. Personalization, personalization engines, and multichannel marketing hubs are moving forwards on Gartner's Hype Cycle for Digital Marketing.

So, is it now time for mar-fi to become a reality? Or will shoppers forever remain frustrated about the gap between their expectations and what personalization can offer? The conclusion must be that even if the relevant technology isn't yet plug-and-play mature, there is no doubt that personalization is a powerful way of increasing the effectiveness of marketing. You may not be able to create a feeling of one-to-one personalization for each and every customer, but, as we shall see, less will do. And anyway, how would it be possible to achieve 100% personalization for customers you don't know that well? Moreover, if you could, how would that make those customers feel?

As we shall see, personalization has also been met with a lot of criticism. First, it is a term that has a lot of ambiguity. Many marketers speak about personalization but they don't necessarily totally agree about what it is and when it is useful. And speaking of 'when' – personalization is not *always* the right tactic, since it complements some business scenarios and challenges substantially better than others. So, to avoid misunderstandings, bad investments, and broken promises, we need more clarity, which the next chapter aims to provide.

CHAPTER 2
WHAT IS THE PROBLEM WITH PERSONALIZATION?

As we mentioned in the previous chapter, the potential problems with personalization are manyfold. First, let's have a look at marketing practitioners. These come in several types, as the field of marketing has become huge since the digital transformation started at the beginning of this millennium. Later in this chapter, we'll look at whether personalization is worth it and how this book aims to contribute by uniting marketers behind a common definition.

THREE BRANCHES OF MARKETERS

Digital marketing started out with three branches. One branch was concerned with building organizations' websites as an online presence and hence was of a fairly technical nature. Keep in mind that this was way before content management systems (CMSs) were invented. Anybody who wanted a homepage had to understand HyperText Markup Language (HTML), which is in its essence a mixture of text and layout. They also had to know a lot of technical stuff about how to put a computer online and make it function as a server to make the HTML files available from other parts of the internet.

CMSs appeared during the early 2000s. These are systems that separate content from presentation and thus make it easy (or at least easier) to build and manage corporate websites and ecommerce stores without having to code any HTML. The whole notion of the user experience (UX) emerged on top of this. UX is all about designing homepages in a user-friendly manner such that users can find what they are looking for and achieve their goals. This whole practice later grew into what we know today as the CMS business, with its web agencies, system integrators, and dedicated UX and digital design agencies.

There was a business purpose behind putting those web pages on the internet as they served as a digital brochure that anyone could find and thus be prompted to get in touch with the company. But due to the technical (rather than human-focused) nature of the early CMS business, these marketing practitioners were less concerned with tallying the results of their efforts via clearly stated business goals and key performance indicators (KPIs) measured in money. Their main driving force was 'doing the right thing' to make the user happy. If they knew who the user of the homepage was, it would be interesting to dynamically show them content on the front page that matched their preferences – or, in the case of ecommerce, show them products that they might like. This was just what the marketers had seen Amazon.com do. So, they were definitely interested in personalization, but from the UX perspective rather than for commercial reasons.

The second branch of marketers was occupied with driving traffic to their company's homepage. To begin with, this meant making sure that the homepage was listed and categorized correctly on the directory pages that later came to be the large search engines (such as Yahoo and ultimately Google). This practice attracted people who were into advertising – not so much the creative and brand-oriented '(m)admen' as those who were responsible for distributing the ads and generating footfall in physical stores. When the internet came along, to begin with these marketers were primarily concerned with getting listings into online directories and subsequently purchasing the premium positions and category captainships. The idea was to make their company stand out and get traffic to its homepage. With the evolution of online directories into proper search engines as we know them today, the main function of these people transitioned to that of buying advertising on search engines and news portals. This branch of marketers ultimately grew to become the ad-tech aspect of marketing, centred on media agencies collaborating with ad agencies and advertisers (companies that advertise).

Since the beginning of the digital era, this branch of marketers has become accustomed to measuring every single exposure and click that an ad generates in order to optimize media spending for the advertiser. However, this has traditionally been at an anonymous statistical level where the individual user or customer cannot necessarily be identified. It is thus conceptually quite far removed from the field of UX. In addition, a large part of advertising is concerned with improving brand awareness and potential customers' feelings towards a brand, so as to boost long-term success and not necessarily drive a purchase here and now. Thus, brand advertisers often measure 'soft' proxy metrics instead of real conversions (i.e. people who click an ad with a potential intention of making a purchase). However, being able to show different ads in different places for different people drives better statistics, no matter which metrics you are looking at. This brand of marketers was therefore definitely also interested in personalization.

The third branch of marketers used to do database marketing. They had a database of known customers with physical addresses and perhaps a little extra demographic information. This made it possible to divide customers into segments (see *Chapter 3*) and send them postal letters (so-called direct mail) to encourage them to buy a certain product or subscribe to a certain magazine or service. Software was developed to automatically print people's names and perhaps even their personal data (such as occupation or title) on the fronts of the envelopes and inside the letters. The idea was to make the communications feel more personal and thus drive higher open rates and conversion rates (as in 'converting' non-customers into customers).

With the advent of email as a common method of communication (for both people and companies), the direct marketing discipline initially evolved into email marketing and then into a more channel-rich form, namely multichannel marketing. Multichannel included email, direct mail (even marketing via fax in some cases), text message marketing, and to some degree online landing pages. Since then, it has evolved to become omnichannel marketing. The term 'personalization' has become a major concern as data collection is now a native part of digital communication and it is easier than ever to imagine and orchestrate bidirectional customer journeys (where customers' interactions with a company determine the next message they are sent). Direct marketers have therefore been using personalization since the beginning.

Some would argue that we've left out the brand marketers here – but there's a good reason for that. Within brand marketing, personalization is of hardly any use. A company has its core brand story and this shouldn't be different for different customers. Thus, it shouldn't be personalized.

So, looking at these three branches within marketing, it is easy to see how each of them should be interested in personalization, since personalization allows marketers to show content to individuals that better fits their preferences and ultimately drives a better UX and better commercial results. However, looking at where they come from, there is also clear potential for them to misunderstand each other and perceive topics and goals very differently. This can lead to confusing conversations and, not surprisingly, sometimes also trouble collaborating on personalization.

IS PERSONALIZATION WORTH IT?

It seems intuitive and logical that personalization creates a better customer experience and that this can lead to an increase in response rates and, ultimately, sales. However, there is still an ongoing discussion about whether personalization is worth it. Is the juice worth the squeeze?

It does, after all, require some amount of work to conceptualize and produce the different content variants needed and to set up the software to do the matching and distribution. And, in addition, there are out-of-pocket expenses for software licences (e.g. for CMSs and marketing automation platforms). This is all needed to make sure that the right people get the most relevant content and that personalization is *effective*.

If you manage this process poorly, then clearly you may waste time and money producing and distributing content variants for customers that make little or even no difference. Personalization has to be not only *effective* but also *efficient*.

In the previous chapter we discussed the hype of personalization and saw how Gartner believes that personalization technology is moving forward through the hype cycle, now reaching the 'plateau of productivity'. But even within Gartner, the aforementioned internal confusion between marketers seems to pop up. In a prediction in 2019, Gartner claimed that by 2025, some 80% of marketers will abandon personalization efforts due to data management issues, poor technology, and difficulties with proving a return on investment (ROI).[1]

Indeed, the idea of there being difficulties around proving ROI resonates with the proxy metrics in use by branding-oriented advertisers (part of the second branch of marketers discussed above). As we shall see in *Part III*, data is truly one of the (if not the) primary prerequisites for making personalization profitable.

Also, reading between the lines, it could be that at least for the authors of the 2019 prediction, Gartner's perception of the term 'personalization' is actually more like so-called hyper-personalization, where every interaction is very personalized. As we shall see in *Chapter 14*, it most likely isn't realistic – nor profitable – to always aim for a hyper-personalized customer experience for all customers.

THE BRANDING SCEPTICS

Personalization has met with criticism not only from research companies but also from within the professional marketing community itself. We get the eerie feeling that sometimes there is an element of click-baiting at play here, but let's see what one prominent article has to say.

Personally, we found it both very interesting and at first glance quite discouraging when, in May 2022, we stumbled upon an article in *Marketing Week* with the title 'Forget Personalization, It's Impossible and It Doesn't Work'.[2] We had just started work on this book and we were met with the claim that personalization is impossible and we should just forget about it. But before abandoning the book project altogether, we decided to actually read the article.

The two authors of the article aren't nobodies. Both have substantial followings on Twitter and LinkedIn and have been working at LinkedIn for a decade or so. In the article, their claim basically seems to be that even though personalization ought to be the best thing since sliced bread:

1. Poor data quality voids the feasibility of personalization altogether
2. Third-party data is broken
3. You'll never get a full picture of any customer
4. It's too expensive to produce one piece of content per end customer

But reading between the lines, we felt the article's focus was primarily on advertising and more specifically brand advertising – a discipline where we fully agree that personalization isn't the obvious choice of tactics. Furthermore, the article primarily uses business-to-business examples to prove that third-party advertising data (we'll learn more about different data types in *Chapter 15*) is broken. Historically, third-party data has been much better at tracking and profiling consumers and thus at supporting business-to-consumer companies in their advertising efforts (although with the latest focus on privacy and with third-party cookies slowly becoming extinct, this also seems to be coming to an end).

So, it seems to us that the authors had their own view on personalization and were of the opinion that within their particular field, personalization wasn't working for them. But it wasn't clear that the headline didn't necessarily apply to all things personalization – and perhaps not even to the authors. On a side note, we can't help but suspect the authors were aware of this and partly wanted to create a headline that would turn heads and make people react. Once an adperson…

The takeaway here is that while these authors had one perception of the topic of personalization, we personally come from different backgrounds – namely, the two other branches of marketing, where first-party customer data and owned media (such as email, web, SMS, and apps) are dominating the scene.

So, having dived deep into the arguments of the sceptics, we decided to continue our book project.

WE NEED A CLEAR DEFINITION OF PERSONALIZATION, NOW

It is clear, then, that there are numerous perceptions of personalization pointing in many different directions all at once. So what, then, is personalization really? Is it a hoax that we should forget about? Or is the hype that technology vendors seem to suggest exists in fact real? What is the true, nuanced picture here?

As marketers, we need this book to gain a better and common understanding of the term 'personalization'. Only then can we avoid the pitfalls of bad and excessive overinvestment in both tech and people, and create truly profitable personalization while keeping customers happy and not jeopardizing long-term business opportunities.

Not until we have this understanding can we expect people outside marketing to make informed decisions about when to invest in personalization as opposed to totally different investment opportunities (such as opening a new store or sourcing or developing other products). Not until we have this understanding can we expect people to take personalization seriously.

CHAPTER 3
DEFINING PERSONALIZATION

So, what might a definition of 'personalization' look like? First of all, let's be clear that in this book we are concerned with the topic of personalized communication: communication that companies initiate primarily from either a marketing or a communications department. This book (including the definitions it offers) could potentially be useful in areas such as product development, research and development, and how a product can be personalized for specific customers. However, this is not the aim of the book, so please consider yourself to have been provided with a hefty disclaimer if you're coming at the book from one of those angles.

During the research process for the book, we came in contact with Dr Tekila Nobile from the University of Lugano in Switzerland, to whom we owe much gratitude for having unravelled the emergence of personalization from an academic perspective. Nobile and her colleague Nadzeya Kalbaska wrote in their article 'An Exploration of Personalization in Digital' (2020) that they too see the problems that arise from the fragmented understanding of personalization. They also see the need for a comprehensive and updated definition of the term:

The lack of common terminology still represents one of the obstacles to fully understand the concept and all its facets.[1]

In their article they describe how personalization isn't a new term – it has been mentioned and used since way before the advent of the internet.

They also go further to describe some of its characteristics.

PERSONALIZATION VS CUSTOMIZATION

It is important to distinguish between personalization and customization. Nobile and Kalbaska discuss this distinction. Although there are several scholars who use the two terms interchangeably, we'd argue that it makes great sense for practitioners to follow the stream of research that distinguishes between the two concepts.

In this stream, set down by Dr Steffen W. Schilke from Plymouth University and colleagues in 2004,[2] **personalization** can be seen as the process through which companies personalize their offering and/or communication with their customers. In contrast, **customization** is a customer-initiated process (hence *custom*ization), where the customer customizes a product (e.g. choosing the colour of a car's interior or having their name printed on sports clothing) or a product view (e.g. by setting explicit criteria for filtering and/or sorting based on the product's properties).

ACTUAL VS PERCEIVED PERSONALIZATION

It also makes sense to distinguish between actual and perceived personalization. **Actual personalization** refers to whether or not the sender of a message has in fact made some kind of personalized modification or is just serving generic content. **Perceived personalization** instead looks at the process from the point of view of the receiver. For instance, a generic set of product recommendations (e.g. bestsellers) could be perceived as personalized if they were presented with the headline 'Especially for you'. This distinction answers the question of whether the end customer has to notice that personalization is going on in order for it to be characterized as 'proper' personalization: the answer is 'no'. Personalization doesn't have to be apparent to the receiver of the message.

IMPLICIT VS EXPLICIT PERSONALIZATION

In this book we shall also distinguish between explicit and implicit personalization. **Explicit personalization** covers cases where it is apparent to the receiver that personalization has taken place. In the case of parametrized personalization – such as 'Hello $FirstName', where all recipients' first names are automatically inserted into an email (for example) – we are talking about explicit personalization. The same goes for the yearly email that Spotify sends its customers where it tallies up how much the individual has used the service, which artists and songs they listened to the most, and so on. In fact, you could argue that any kind of invoice or bill is explicitly personalized. Explicit personalization can also take place without parametrization – for example, on the headline level, where it is clear which segment (see below) of customers the sender has in mind and is personalizing the communication to them.

Implicit personalization, on the other hand, is more subtle. It can easily be the right tactic when addressing touchy subjects such as pregnancy, sexuality, divorce, or even death. During the research for this book, an expert committee discussed how a pension company would always tread very carefully and communicate very subtly (if at all) if there was an indication in the data suggesting that a customer had been through a divorce. It is always worth remembering the classic example of the American retailer Target, which suggested pregnancy-related products to a minor.[3] Her father was furious and called them to complain. They gave him an excuse and explained that it was just the algorithm suggesting products based on previous purchases. Later it turned out that the minor was in fact pregnant. The lesson from this story is that it wasn't wrong for Target to suggest these products, but it should have been more discreet and not put them in the primary position within its recommendations.

TARGETING

Explicit personalization almost always takes place on so-called owned media (web, app, email, SMS, etc.) and very rarely in advertising. This is due to the following facts. First, parametrization in advertising is impossible. Second, you cannot really be sure who will be looking at an ad. Third, explicit personalization in advertising would also come across as super-creepy to most people. We've only ever seen one explicitly personalized ad. This was a Facebook ad that addressed the fact that one of the authors hadn't completed his purchase at a ski-apparel merchant. He actually did go back and complete his purchase. Because of the ad? Not in this case – but for other customers this could have been the determining factor.

When companies use personalization on communication channels where parametrization with personal data isn't possible (e.g. advertising), it is often referred to as **targeting**. Advertising platforms commonly gather insights and allow advertisers to segment their messages based on these insights. It is also possible for advertisers to match their company's own customer data (first-party data) with that of the advertising platform, and thus achieve much more precision.

In advertising on digital paid media, using first-party data to define a so-called audience pretty much sets the bar for how personalized advertising can become. The only way to improve on this is to use tools for product retargeting, which is a way of exposing customers to the exact product they were close to buying.

SEGMENTATION VS PERSONALIZATION – NOT A BINARY DISTINCTION

A topic that was heavily debated in the expert committee meetings that made up part of the research for this book was the distinction between segmentation and personalization. As *Part II* of this book will discuss, **segmentation** is something you do to your customer database. It involves dividing your customers into ever smaller segments to allow you to communicate different things to different people at different times.

If you insert recipients' first names within a piece of content intended for a specific segment, then everybody seems to concur that you are doing personalization. If, however, you don't parametrize anything in the message and it is generic for the segment, then some would argue that you aren't doing personalization but merely segmentation. So, in this light, implicit personalization (as described above) would in fact fit this description and thus be segmentation. Imagine, then, that you set up so many criteria for your segments that they end up being very small indeed. When are the segments small enough for everyone to agree that we are talking about personalization?

As we shall explore in *Part II*, classic segmentation is not the only type of insight you should be using when working with personalization. Behavioural data collected in real time from customers' interactions with your digital platforms and assets has great significance in terms of enabling you to decide whom to send to and when. In essence, this is also a way of segmenting your customer database, albeit very granularly. None of the experts who took part in the research process for this book argued that a generic message sent at the right individualized time (e.g. an email sent to all customers with a credit card expiring in five days) wasn't personalization. We even agreed that *not* sending something could be regarded as personalization. It can hardly get more implicit than that.

It is clear that the distinction between personalization and segmentation is blurry when taken to the extreme. So, for the sake of clarity, we shall treat segmentation as a term that lies within the umbrella term of personalization.

TWO ACADEMIC DEFINITIONS OF PERSONALIZATION

Having covered these important aspects and distinctions related to personalization, it's time to visit some actual definitions and come to a conclusion about which definition the Bowtie of Personalization is built upon. First, let's briefly visit the definition that Gartner suggests:

Personalization is a process that creates a relevant, individualized interaction between two parties designed to enhance the experience of the recipient.[4]

We agree with Gartner that personalization is a process and also that there are two parties involved. But otherwise we find the definition too narrow.

First of all, creating a relevant experience will indeed be a goal of the company, but it is solely up to the recipient to decide whether something is relevant or not. And, as we concluded above, this decision is not an 'either–or' and doesn't even have to be a conscious one. Our second point of critique centres on the word 'individualized'. Since personalization can happen implicitly and at the segment level, this seems out of place in the definition.

Last but not least, the sole focus on enhancing the experience of the recipient seems slightly altruistic, as any marketer is (or should be) out to create value for their company – not just enhance the experience of the recipient. So, at least as a practitioner's definition, Gartner's seems too narrow, as it won't always pay off to invest in individualized communication for the sole purpose of enhancing the customer's experience. As we shall see in

Chapter 14, companies should focus on key parts of the customer journey in their personalization efforts, otherwise it may not be worth the effort.

We shall once again draw upon the work of Tekila Nobile, this time writing with Lorenzo Cantoni, for an alternative definition:

[Personalization is] a dynamic process in which an object is changed for an individual in order to provide added value for the individual herself/himself. Such a process, which takes place in a given context, can be user- or firm-driven. The object, either tangible or intangible, is changed in dimensions at a number of states. The individual either provides information about her/himself, or the information is inferred by the change maker. According to some, personalization and customization are different concepts. Customization is then characterized by an active contribution from an individual, up to her/his involvement in the co-design of a product.[5]

If we start at the end of this definition, then we are confronted with the ambiguity between personalization and customization. As outlined above, for the sake of clarity and general good sense in distinguishing between a customer-initiated and a company-initiated process, we prefer to keep the two terms apart. Moving one step further back in the definition, we meet the term 'information'. In day-to-day marketing jargon, this is referred to as 'data' – either explicit data (voluntarily submitted by the recipient) or insights 'inferred' (perhaps from other data sources). This part of the definition fits with the commonly used terminology of predictive analytics and how algorithms can indeed infer propensities or degrees to which a certain statement holds true for a specific individual. How certain are we that a customer is going through a divorce? If they haven't specifically submitted that data to our company then we're better off not addressing it directly – edge cases aside.

Moving further back in the definition, the 'object' of personalization is usually referred to as 'content' within the marketing discipline. It can, however, also be functionality. For example, should a specific feature be visible for a specific customer of an online bank? The idea of changing content across several dimensions fits beautifully with the Bowtie of Personalization, as we shall see in *Part II*. And the reference to 'tangible or intangible' objects could refer to the fact that the exclusion of a specific customer from a certain message is also a form of personalization.

Finally, the first part of the definition is the soul of personalization: it is used because the sender believes that it will create better value for the recipient. Again, however, we feel that the goal of profiting from personalization gets lost in this definition.

A PRACTITIONER'S DEFINITION OF PERSONALIZATION

One company in which personalization is a core strategy is Netflix. At a conference in Gothenburg, Sweden, in 2022, Gibson Biddle recounted how he carried out several personalization experiments during his time as Vice President of Product for Netflix.[6] His framework for creating value in this role involves focusing on three core points:

- Delighting the customer
- Making things that are hard to copy
- Margin enhancement

Biddle labels this his DHM framework (with the 'H' coming from 'hard').[7] Among other tactics, such as having unique content, personalization ticks all three boxes in this framework. We believe the margin enhancement point beautifully underlines the duality of value creation – for both the customer and the company – to a much larger extent than do the two previously visited definitions.

On the basis of the above definitions and with the discussed distinctions in mind, we propose the following practitioner's definition of personalization:

Personalization is a distinct communication tactic that aims to create better immediate and future business value by showing or hiding specific content to recipients in a way that is expected to align with insights into their explicit or inferred preferences.

Let's break this definition down. First of all, personalization is one of many potential communication tactics, hence the term 'distinct'. The vast majority of practitioners use it as a tactic, but there are also examples where personalization is used as a core strategy. This is the case for companies such as Amazon, Facebook, and Netflix. In general, if your product is 100% digital, then personalization stands a higher chance of becoming a strategic differentiator.

Personalization is often used within marketing, but not all communication prone to personalization is related to marketing-specific goals. Hence, we use the term 'communication tactic' and not 'marketing tactic'. The message that creates the most value for recipient and company alike may very well be a non-marketing-related message. If, for instance, a customer has had a bad experience with a certain service, then the next best message will most likely be one that explains what went wrong and what has been done to avoid this happening again. It's not marketing a new product or a potential upsell (which could easily come across as pushy and aggressive).

When practitioners work with personalization, they have a purpose in mind. As long as the value creation is mutual for recipient and company, it's fine to enhance the customer experience. The overall purpose, however, is to create *business* value. This can be short term ('immediate') or long term ('future'). For example, in the short term, a company might be chasing conversions on a specific campaign in order to meet short-term targets. This can mean repeating a certain offer multiple times – but not to the point where it jeopardizes future business value (e.g. if the recipient begins to perceive the messages as spam, resulting in decreased brand perception and trust – or even causing the recipient to choose to unsubscribe from further communication by revoking their consent to marketing).

The idea of 'showing or hiding specific content' refers to the fact that choosing *not* to show or send content to a recipient can sometimes be beneficial for long-term business value. If the chances of a specific recipient finding a specific offer relevant are slim to none, then it's better not to show (let alone send) that offer to that recipient so as not to create noise and annoyance. As we shall see in *Chapter 8*, content comes in many forms, and these can easily coexist or be part of the same customer experience, for instance when a person looks at a website, an app, and an email.

The term 'recipients' refers to the fact that there is a receiving end of personalized communication. The company is sending or showing the content and recipients are receiving it. Of course, interactions do take place where the 'recipients' submit personal information, and thus these interactions resemble mutual conversations. Note that 'recipients' is in the plural because personalization always has the goal of scaling personalized experiences to as many recipients as possible in order to maximize the value gained from the effort.

The last part of the definition refers to how the specifically shown content is expected to align with the preferences of the recipients. We use 'expected' because there can only be one judge of whether alignment has been achieved – namely, the recipient. No matter how much data is collected, marketers generally have only vague impressions of the contexts and the intentions of their recipients (unless these are explicitly stated, of course). Nevertheless, preferences can still be inferred to a greater or lesser degree based on data collection and advanced analytics, and this can certainly still create value for both parties.

PERSONALIZATION IS NOT AN 'EITHER-OR'

Our definition of personalization is fairly wide, as indeed are the other two definitions discussed above. Some practitioners might argue that it is *too* wide compared with their perception of personalization. However, we believe that marketers would benefit from uniting to understand, respect, and connect with each other's definitions to present a stronger position and more robust results to senior management.

Thus, our definition is open to many forms of personalization, both implicit and explicit, and on both owned and paid media. So, to conclude this chapter, personalization is not a binary thing but more a question of degrees. This means that, for instance, choosing to show ads to an audience that Facebook believes algorithmically matches your best customers is an act of personalization. It is definitely not the most explicit example of personalization, and the people seeing the ad will probably never realize that it wasn't just random coincidence they saw it. However, it is still personalization.

CHAPTER 4
WHY DOES PERSONALIZATION WORK?

Though it may seem like the most natural thing in the world that people will engage more with content and messages that are aligned with their preferences, we'd still like to dwell a little on *why* personalization works. Tekila Nobile and Nadzeya Kalbaska put it like this in their article 'An Exploration of Personalization in Digital Communication':

Individuals are more likely to embrace information that is attitude-consistent and prefer information that aligns with their perspective. … Messages that are relevant to consumers should increase their motivation to process the information.[1]

But why is that so? As explained by Ville Salonen and Heikki Karjaluoto from the University of Jyväsklä in Finland,[2] the effects of personalization can be attributed to evolutionary psychology and what is called the fundamental motives framework. This was originally described in 2013 by Vladas Griskevicius from the University of Minnesota and Douglas T. Kenrick from Arizona State University.[3] The idea of 'fundamental motives' refers to what it is that we humans are actually looking for – in other words, and relating this back to our definition of personalization in *Chapter 3*, what consumers' most profound *preferences* really are.

The fundamental motives include:

- Evading physical harm
- Avoiding disease
- Making friends
- Attaining status
- Acquiring a mate
- Caring for family

At any given time, a range of these motives will be active for an individual. For example, if an individual is browsing for clothes on a fashion website, then 'attaining status' and 'acquiring a mate' could be their active fundamental motives. Half an hour later, their active fundamental motives may have changed and they may be going to the gym to 'avoid disease' and 'make friends'. As Salonen and Karjaluoto put it:

The currently active motive shapes preferences and guides decision processes.[4]

Personalization works when you communicate about a specific thing that a customer profoundly wants. People vary over time in terms of how relevant each motive is for them, and there are certainly some people who tend to be driven by some of the motives more than by others.

So, if you want to succeed with personalization, it makes sense to keep these fundamental motives in mind. You can think about how your customer insights relate back to the motives and consider which ones could be active in the moment for each individual. If you are selling a car, for instance, does the browsing pattern of the customer mostly indicate that they are looking for status or interested in caring for their family? The content you choose to present – such as suggested car models or descriptive text – should match the customer's fundamental motive in order to maximize your impact.

Some motives will be more continuously active for some individuals and thus make up what could be called their 'permanent preferences' or their personality. This will all become clearer when we discuss customer insights as part of the Bowtie of Personalization in *Part II*.

WHEN THINGS GET CREEPY

Unfortunately, personalization efforts can backfire and have the opposite effect to their purpose of creating immediate and future business results. One of the most discussed topics in this regard is when things get creepy and personalization is perceived by people as stepping over their personal boundaries. The question is, what is it that makes your customers feel that way?

Today, many consumers expect personalization. According to the study *State of the Connected Customer*, 66% of consumers expect companies to understand their unique needs and expectations, and 52% expect *all* offers to be personalized.[5]

McKinsey takes this idea one step further and claims that consumers are now at a point where they *demand* personalization. According to McKinsey's own *Next in Personalization 2021 Report*, 71% of consumers now expect companies to deliver personalized interactions and 76% get frustrated when this doesn't happen.[6] Yet it is still possible for marketers to take things too far and come across as creepy.

WHEN DO CONSUMERS FIND PERSONALIZATION CREEPY?

Consumers tend to report creepiness in three main cases. First, they feel creeped out if they perceive that they are being stalked by mindless repetitions of the same advertisement – like some hollow echo of their browsing pattern. This is especially the case if they feel that the advertiser should be able to tell that they are no longer in the market for the specific product. An example of this that we hear mentioned over and over again is Hotels.com, which has been told to keep sending emails to people about, for example, hotels in Rome several weeks after they've returned from there. Many people enjoy visiting Rome – but most people don't enjoy it multiple weekends in a row.

The second way of creeping people out is if you use customer data or insights that the customer wasn't aware you had. This can happen when the data comes from a third-party data source, the consent wasn't clearly stated at the time of collection, or the customer has forgotten that they gave you the data.

For most people it will come as no surprise if they receive an email that follows up on a specific online purchase. The customer knows that the retailer has this data and as such the retailer can use it very explicitly. Thus, it is possible to mention the products bought (e.g. by suggesting how-to videos to help customers optimize their use of the products) without anyone feeling creeped out. If, however, customers are not aware that the retailer has collected specific data and that this is used for explicit personalization, many will find it creepy. An example of this could be tracking individual page visits on a website. This collection of data is possible through either a server-side or a first-party browser cookie. If the retailer then sends the customer an email explicitly mentioning that the brand knows the customer has browsed 18 variants of sexy underwear and suggesting that the customer look at even more such underwear, this email would most likely be perceived as creepy.

That said, some customers might not find it creepy – it all depends on the individual customer as well as how the brand presents itself and how it is perceived. Customers of Victoria's Secret might not find this creepy at all. People in China might not find it creepy either, since they are used to being surveilled by the Chinese government. People in Germany most likely would find it creepy, as Germans tend to value privacy very dearly. The notion of creepiness is also a cultural thing.

The underwear example touches upon the third way of creeping people out – namely, addressing topics that the customer finds it inappropriate to share or discuss with the brand. Imagine you're having a conversation with a real person you just met at a dinner party. You would need to know and trust this person before you started to discuss sexy underwear or how you felt about a potential divorce. Marketers (and new acquaintances at dinner parties) should tread carefully when addressing such topics, as well as when revealing their sources for the insights behind their questions and suggestions (see *Figure 4*). First of all, make sure you have trust and rapport. You could then hint at the topic and bring it up in passing or indirectly. Implicit personalization, as described in *Chapter 3*, is your friend here.

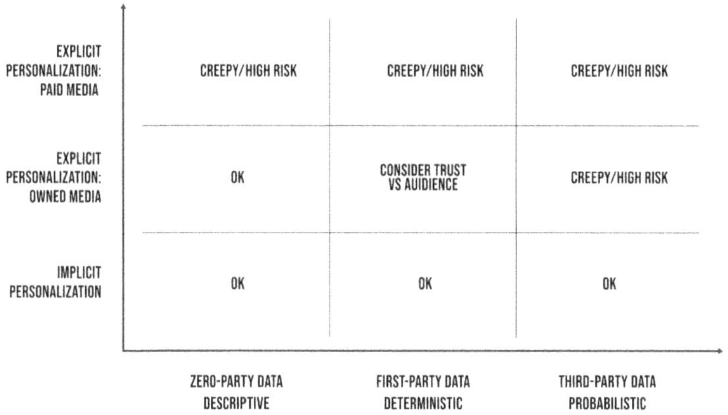

	ZERO-PARTY DATA DESCRIPTIVE	FIRST-PARTY DATA DETERMINISTIC	THIRD-PARTY DATA PROBABILISTIC
EXPLICIT PERSONALIZATION: PAID MEDIA	CREEPY/HIGH RISK	CREEPY/HIGH RISK	CREEPY/HIGH RISK
EXPLICIT PERSONALIZATION: OWNED MEDIA	OK	CONSIDER TRUST VS AUIDIENCE	CREEPY/HIGH RISK
IMPLICIT PERSONALIZATION	OK	OK	OK

Figure 4. The data types used for personalization and their impact on how consumers perceive creepiness.

PERSONALIZED VS PERSONAL

The discussion of creepiness relates to the difference between communication being personalized or personal. The feeling of something being **personal** belongs to the receiver, and as a marketer you should be careful not to be more personal in your communication than your receivers are comfortable with. Most customers don't want an intimate relationship with brands – you are not their new best friend and won't become so either. So, for us personally, please stop writing emails to us that say your brand 'loves us' and how excited you are about fulfilling our orders.

It does help if you combine personalization with **personification**, though, which means sending (or pretending to be sending) the email from a real person. You could use the name of your founder, your head of ecommerce, your chief evangelist, or another appropriate person, and insert their picture or a scanned signature. Also make sure the email address doesn't start with 'noreply' and that replies to the email actually do go to the person on whose behalf it was sent. This will make the message feel more personal and, in our experience, can improve results.

Most people will still figure out that these messages are not sent manually by a real person, especially if the email is branded and there are a lot of graphics and layout in it. However, they will still expect a real person to be behind the words and mentally hold that person accountable for the content.

B2B BUSINESS DEVELOPMENT – PRETENDING TO BE PERSONAL?

In business-to-business (B2B) – and especially in meeting booking scenarios – there are various software tools that can be used to do automated outreach and personalize emails and LinkedIn messages. In these cases, it is not really possible to brand the message through layout and graphics. As such, the recipient can't tell by looking at it whether it's a manually sent message from a real person or whether it's an automated message. So, whether by design or not, these messages pretend to be personal.

Some of these attempts to do outreach and personalize messages in this fashion are quite horrible and assume way too much about the potential buying intent of the recipient. Often they get the industry or the role of the recipient wrong. If you are in any kind of role with a budget, we bet you've received tons of these messages already. Perhaps it's more annoying than creepy, but it's still personalization.

CREEPY PERSONALIZATION OR JUST A COINCIDENCE?

You've probably heard people saying that they've talked about a certain topic or product, only to shortly afterwards be exposed to advertisements about the particular product on Facebook or Google. This brings up the suspicion that the tech giants are listening in on our physical conversations and are using this knowledge in their advertising. Especially if people have a Google Nest speaker or an Amazon Echo or Alexa in the house, the suspicion grows. The speaker is always listening (unless it is switched off), but it is supposed to only react and process data when it is called out (as in 'Hey Google').

There have been several stories in the media concerning this topic – and in particular, Amazon Echo has been accused of recording and even sending sound recordings in unfortunate circumstances. One woman in Portland, Oregon, claimed that her Amazon Echo had secretly recorded a conversation and sent the recording to a contact on her husband's phone. Amazon said this was the result of an 'unlikely' series of events.[7]

We're not the ones to decide whether Amazon, Google, or Apple are really listening in on our conversations, although don't Google and Amazon already have enough data on their customers to determine with some accuracy which products they'd be interested in, without having to listen in on their conversations? What we will say is that we see people's readiness to believe their devices are listening as a clear sign that consumers have come to expect personalization everywhere. Sometimes, therefore, lucky coincidences are perceived as the results of personalization.

CHAPTER 5
MARKETING WITHOUT PERSONALIZATION

In *Chapter 3* we settled on a definition of personalization that all marketing practitioners should be able to comprehend and will hopefully find useful. As we concluded, the definition is fairly wide. In fact, it is so wide that it may be hard to imagine marketing without any form of personalization or at least some sort of customer segmentation (which we concluded is one form of personalization).

Imagine, for instance, that you are marketing a high-end shoe brand and are planning a campaign run entirely on physical out-of-home media. Obviously, you are likely to be happy to pay more to have your ads displayed on bus stops in neighbourhoods where wealthier families tend to live. And you will perhaps not use any budget at all for neighbourhoods where less wealthy people live. Since you will then be indirectly choosing some customers over others, this is essentially segmentation and thus also personalization to some degree. Haven't marketers then always used some kind of segmentation and personalization?

In this chapter, with the purpose of understanding personalization on an even deeper level, we shall explore how marketing looks when we take personalization out of the equation. As the example above shows, in real life this may not be possible at all, but the exercise will bring us closer to comprehending what personalization isn't – or which parts of marketing it cannot make up for and that still need to be taken into account when striving for profitability. As the definition says, personalization is a *distinct* communication tactic – not the *only* communication tactic.

THE PERSONALIZATION-VALUE EQUATION

Marketing has always been a commercial discipline. In essence, it's the third function needed in a company. First you need a product, then you need salespeople, and finally, when their efforts are no longer scaling, roughly put that's where marketing comes in. So, marketing has always been about creating value. But how is value then created?

Basically, value is created by taking your value proposition and presenting it in an engaging way to as many people as possible. This is illustrated in the following equation:

$$\text{VALUE} = \text{PROPOSITION} \times \text{FORMAT} \times \text{REACH}$$

SHORT- OR LONG-TERM VALUE CREATION

In much the same way as personalization does, marketing can focus on creating value with either a short-term or a long-term perspective. Short-term marketing is often referred to as **performance marketing** and advertising for a long-term effect is commonly referred to as **branding**. The two aren't mutually exclusive since branding campaigns will often also drive sales here and now, and vice versa:

- **Performance marketing: chasing short-term conversions** – Performance marketing is focused on proposing some kind of action – often a purchase – that the audience is recommended to take. It can happen either on paid media (such as search engine marketing, e.g. on Google or Bing) or on paid social media (such as Facebook, Instagram, or TikTok). There will often be a direct link to suggested products or even the option of browsing the products right there on the advertising platform. Performance marketing can obviously also take place on owned media, such as in a newsletter full of this week's offers or the products of the season. Classic measures of performance marketing include click-through rates, conversion rates, and return on advertising spend.

- **Branding: affecting how people feel about your brand** – Whereas performance marketing is focused on encouraging the customer to take a specific action here and now, branding is focused on making customers feel something. This might mean encouraging customers to just feel more familiar with the brand and how it looks, or to associate the brand with certain experiences, moods, or occasions. Classic measures of branding include brand awareness, brand consideration, brand preference, and brand usage. Another option is brand associations.

USING STRONG VALUE PROPOSITIONS FOR EASIER MARKETING

Moving into the parts of the equation that create the value, we first encounter the term **proposition**. What is it that your company is offering and how is this attractive to customers? What products or services are you proposing to your customers?

A proposition can be more or less attractive for a certain customer or group of customers. If you're digging holes all day then you might consider a company selling shovels to have quite a good value proposition. If you want to minimize the economic risk of getting robbed or crashing your car then insurance would be an interesting value proposition.

All propositions have a flipside, however, namely how much friction is involved in taking advantage of the value proposition. Friction could relate to either monetary or practical concerns. Is the offering very expensive? And how easy is it to take advantage of?

A Ferrari may seem very attractive to many people – but it's considered expensive for the vast majority. A cheap health club membership that still includes personal trainers, swimming facilities, and a sauna will seem very attractive for most people – but if the physical location is too far from your home or work address, there will still be too much friction for the value proposition to be attractive.

The proposition can therefore be thought of as attraction divided by friction:

Needless to say, a strong value proposition will make marketing considerably easier. And personalization will not make up for a poor value proposition.

GETTING THE FORMAT RIGHT TO ENGAGE YOUR AUDIENCE

Value propositions don't normally sell themselves. They need to be presented in ways that your audience will notice and, hopefully, remember. To do this, you need a strong **format**. Creativity is key here, taking the form of humour, emotions, or elements of surprise. The more creativity that you can put into a format, the more your value proposition will get noticed and remembered, and the more value you'll eventually get from your marketing.

Again, there's a flipside. A strong format is often expensive to produce. If you hire superstar Katy Perry to dance around in a cartoon-like plastic-fantastic environment while singing and ordering take-out from your company, then you will probably get a lot of attention and potentially also value – but most likely she won't do it for free. A strong format often – but not always – comes at a high cost. We can therefore consider format to consist of creativity divided by the cost of production:

Sometimes a high production cost is worth it. An expensive-looking high-end ad can create an aura around your value proposition, giving your audience the feeling that your product is equally high end. This can enable you to create value with your marketing even though the friction (i.e. price) of your value proposition is high.

Personalization does not void the need for thinking about format. If your marketing and communication are consistently boring, forgettable, unengaging, and potentially even insensitive, then it doesn't matter how good you are at segmenting your customer database.

ACHIEVING MORE VALUE VIA HIGH REACH

An expensive ad for a good value proposition is wasted if no one sees it. Naturally, **reaching** a large audience is key to creating value. But reach is not just reach. Some channels will provide you with better engagement than others. A carefully crafted post by a trusted and well-followed influencer will generate much more engagement than will a display advertising campaign on Google Display Network. A Google Search advert will also beat the display advert in terms of engagement. The display advert loses because consumers have become more and more immune to this form of marketing. Both the influencer marketing post and the Google Search advert will likely come at a much higher cost than the display advert. But the engagement will be substantially higher! This is shown in the following version of the equation:

In much the same way that personalization doesn't remove the need to decide on the right proposition or to make sure you present it in an engaging format, personalization won't compensate for poor reach.

Sometimes reach suffers when personalization is applied. If done properly, however, the increase in engagement should greatly make up for this –

especially if you use the right combination of software and skills to merge your insights and content efficiently. The overall message is that you shouldn't sacrifice your ability to reach a lot of customers by being too narrow with unscalable hyper-personalization.

ADDING *EXTRA* VALUE TO YOUR MARKETING THROUGH PERSONALIZATION

If you are good at reaching a lot of potential customers with an attractive proposition in a strong format, then you have a lot of things working out for you already. Personalization will then enable you to create additional value in your marketing communication:

$$\text{VALUE} = \text{PROPOSITION} \times \text{FORMAT} \times \text{REACH} \times \text{PERSONALIZATION}$$

Countless studies have examined and quantified the potential effects of personalization. Personally, we're big fans of how McKinsey's authors present the topic in the *Next in Personalization 2021 Report.*[1] In the study they divide companies into different archetypes based on their go-to-market (GTM) models and how directly each company interacts with its customers. The GTM models that benefit the least from personalization are the ones with the least direct customer relationships, such as fast-moving consumer goods and consumer packaged goods. These companies report that they see an average of 5–10% of their revenue coming from personalized marketing actions or tactics. At the other end of the spectrum lie the born-digital direct-to-consumer companies, with a staggering 25% (approximately) of their revenue attributed to personalized actions or tactics. The potential of 'adding' personalization for non-practitioners will thus be:

$$1 / (1-25\%) = 1.33 \rightarrow \text{A 33\% UPLIFT}$$

And this is only the average – the actual potential is even bigger. As we shall see in *Chapter 16*, there are good reasons to keep in mind the potential spread in the effect that can be achieved with personalization, and how this spread correlates with the GTM models suggested by McKinsey.

With a potential uplift of more than 33% for companies with certain GTM models, it makes sense that marketers and tech vendors are looking into how they can apply or help to apply personalization to their customer experience. In *Part II* of this book, we shall explore a novel practitioner's perspective on personalization. This perspective will serve as a guide for how you as a marketer can move closer to manifesting this potential as real money.

PART TWO
A PRACTITIONER'S VIEW ON PERSONALIZATION

CHAPTER 6
THE BOWTIE OF PERSONALIZATION

Kirsten works at PureGym as the Head of CRM in Denmark. Her most important task is to minimize churn from the company's rather large base of health club members. From a churn analysis report carried out earlier in the year, she has confirmation that if a member does not show up at the gym for more than two weeks, this constitutes a churn risk – which she will want to address. One week's absence from the gym can happen to anybody, she thinks to herself, but two weeks of absence can easily break an otherwise healthy habit. Members who have been away for 14 days or more could – consciously or not – be at a decisive moment of truth as to whether they'll continue working out at PureGym. Today there aren't that many members who fit the criteria, but Kirsten knows that each and every day there will be other members who do. So, when she sets up the corresponding communication flow, she's confident that this will create great value over time.

Thinking about the customer personas the company created last year, Kirsten realizes that they need to craft multiple variants of the reactivation message depending on which segment they are communicating to. Young people working out to look amazing on the beach need different arguments than do senior citizens who work out for the sake of ageing healthily. Kirsten makes a note asking the copywriter to carefully write messages for each major segment as well as a default variant for the remaining customers. 'And please remember that we can't really know for sure if they are considering leaving us – so be a little subtle,' she adds. All major communication channels also need to be considered, so the copywriter will craft all the copy needed for emails, push notifications, the app, the website, and even the paid ads that Kirsten plans in order to show the members they simply cannot afford to lose. Graphics will be made accordingly. For each segment, she decides to define an inspirational content block with selected exercises and classes that match each segment, for example hardcore strength exercises for the young men and gentle mind–body classes for the elderly women. The content blocks will be featured in emails, in the app, and on the website for each individual.

The above scenario illustrates how personalization might take place in a health club such as PureGym. In this case, the Head of CRM, Kirsten, carefully matches the insights she has about both moments of truth and segmentation with content such as creative reactivation messages and inspirational feeds of suggested exercises and classes. This maki cube of supposedly customer-relevant communication is then produced at a channel-agnostic level (an omnichannel level) before it is applied in an automated communication flow that spans the most important communication channels between PureGym and its members. This is a textbook example of using personalization to optimize the feeling of relevance and reduce membership churn.

The scenario touches upon two key elements that are key to succeeding with personalization – namely insights and content. Broken down further, the insights consist of both the dynamic moment of truth (in the form of the member inactivity) and the rather static customer segments (both young and old members). The content consists of both carefully crafted creative messages and curated feeds of content with recommended classes. The beauty of the example also lies in the omnichannel approach to both the production and the distribution of the messages across owned and paid media. In owned media the inactivity can be addressed fairly explicitly, whereas in paid media the reactivation message needs to be a bit more implicit and subtle so as not to be perceived as creepy.

These four elements of insight and content together form the Bowtie of Personalization (see *Figure 5*), which serves as this book's main model for understanding the different forms of personalization. As we'll cover in the following chapters, each of the four 'corners' of the bowtie has its rightful place and purpose. Each one plays the main role in some areas of personalization and a smaller role in others.

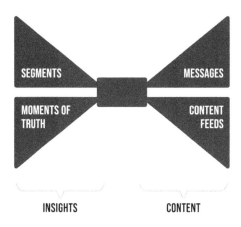

Figure 5. The Bowtie of Personalization

A GLIMPSE OF HYPER-PERSONALIZATION – WHAT'S 'KNOT' TO LIKE?

If all four corners of the bowtie are in play at the same time, this is pretty much the most personalized a piece of communication can become. Naturally the insights can, over time, become more precise through better data collection and algorithms. The content can also become more creative, and you can have more content variants matching more segments. Eventually the customer experience in this case becomes what is often referred to as 'hyper-personalization'.

The amount of work you put into tying this beautiful knot will be worth it if you use it for the most important parts of your customer journey and craft a personalized and memorable experience. Imagine the customer journey as one very long piece of cloth with a knot of hyper-personalization for each critical moment along the way, so that you have a chain of bows placed at appropriate points along your customer journey.

In the case of PureGym, one of the most important business goals is to reduce member churn, and the most dominant customer insight in assessing the risk of churn for a single member is inactivity (as in not having been to the gym). This is why it makes sense for the PureGym team to do everything in their power to create a personalized and memorable customer experience for all customers who happen to be inactive – for one reason or another – in order to reactivate as many members as possible in an automated and relevant way.

For an online grocery retailer, the most important part of the customer journey could be getting new customers to make three purchases within a month. For a charity it could be getting a donor to sign a recurring donation subscription. These moments are where you should focus your personalization efforts. They are where you should tie the most beautiful bowtie knots that you can.

For the less critical parts of the customer journey, you can justify a more general and less personalized experience. It won't be profitable to aim for hyper-personalization at every single touchpoint with customers.

DRAMATIZING THE KNOT IN THE BOWTIE

Doubling down on the knot in the bowtie will help you to create the impact that you're after, but it is also the perfect way to communicate what personalization is all about and what kind of customer experience you are out to create. So why not dramatize it and put it into a narrative in much the same way as we have in the case study at the beginning of this chapter? Why not make this narrative into an animated video that can be shown at internal town halls, to new employees, and to all team members who are trying to make this narrative a reality? Since the dawn of time, human beings have gathered around the campfire listening to narratives and seeing themselves in them. A dramatized narrative about how personalization can create better customer experiences and business results has the power to convey personalization on both a logical level and an emotional level like almost nothing else.

TRUE PERSONALIZATION MAGIC HAPPENS BEFORE THE CHANNELS

There's an old saying that is often mentioned when the conversation turns to personalization: 'personalization is about sending the right message to the right person at the right time and through the right channel'. So, if we take a closer look at the Bowtie of Personalization, you could argue that it covers the content of this sentence to a large extent. However, the 'right channel' part is not included. Why is that so?

As individual consumers, we don't have *one* relevant channel. We cannot *only* be reached on the *right channel*. We all wish we were better at using ad-blockers, unsubscribing from uninteresting newsletters and app notifications, and doing *some* digital detoxing, but we're most often not. The same goes for the vast majority of people out there. Also, people often need to see the same message multiple times in order for it to sink in. Exactly how many times per person cannot be absolutely determined – but engaging formats will, of course, bring this number down.

Communication channels cater to different formats and thus each have their own rules of engagement. For instance, you'd rarely use the same content on TikTok as you would in a personalized email. As a marketer, however, you should use the Bowtie of Personalization to at least mentally decide who should be exposed to which content at which given time. And remember that the core of the message can essentially be the same no matter how different the formats.

CENTRAL MANAGEMENT OF INSIGHTS AND CONTENT DRIVES EFFICIENT PERSONALIZATION

As we shall cover in *Chapter 14*, the more centralized your management of your content, the more efficiently you'll be able to execute personalized communication across channels and thus create better results with less effort (see *Figure 6*). Conversely, the more that content is built into or created for each specific channel or platform, the more cumbersome it is to both create and maintain. Although it can feel arbitrary and detached to put together a message without having a specific channel in mind, it is necessary for optimal efficiency.

The same logic applies to how you determine insights, in the form of both customer segments and moments of truth, and how they match the specific content pieces. If this logic is built into each channel, then personalization across channels can be very hard to both build and manage.

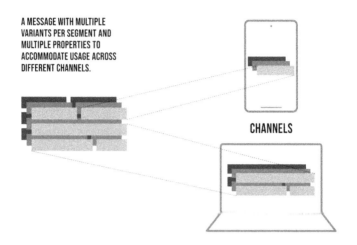

Figure 6. Ideally, personalization happens before a message is applied to a specific channel; the message will appear differently in each channel.

THE ART OF THE POSSIBLE

As not all channels or platforms offer the ability to publish content to specific audiences from a central content hub, it is, of course, the art of the possible that is at play here. If your tools and channels do not offer central orchestration across the board, then less will do, of course – it will just make the process more cumbersome. The results you achieve could still be worth the trouble, though.

WEBSITES AND APPS MASH IT UP

On inbound platforms (web, apps, and even in-store), many types of content are visible at the same time. So, more often than not, multiple content feeds and multiple messages will appear simultaneously. Not all of these will be personalized, however, as these platforms carry general information that needs to be available for all customers and also cater to the anonymous visitor. Over time, however, you should strive to increase the degree of personalization on digital platforms by motivating customer identification though a persistent log-in and subsequent data collection of interactions and purchases. An ever-relevant example is to try logging out (yes, you're most likely already logged in) of Amazon and notice how different the website appears. This serves as a testimony to how different a digital platform experience can be because of personalization.

DECIDING ON YOUR COMMUNICATION CHANNELS

We've established, then, that consumers don't have *one* right channel – and, as will be explored further below, messages often have to be repeated in order to affect decisions. These factors have great implications for how you select which communication channels to work with in your personalization efforts. Optimizing cost will be the guiding principle for deciding which channels to choose.

OWNED MEDIA BEFORE PAID MEDIA

As a rule of thumb, owned media is the preferred choice for personalized communication since it will enable you to control your costs to a much higher degree than is possible on paid media. Showing a personalized message on your website and in your app will generally not cost you anything. Similarly, sending emails and push notifications will generally have a very low transaction cost. The same cannot quite be said for SMS, which carries a small fee, and certainly not for direct mail, which is considerably more expensive.

If you can efficiently distribute your message to the right individuals through owned media and you see that this has the intended effect, then it makes sense not to try to further expose these customers to this message – and certainly not on paid media. You might, however, still be missing the intended reaction from your customers (indeed, some audiences are using email less than others[1]). If so, you'll have to decide how much it is worth for you to use paid media to further try and drive the desired action. As we shall later see, this is also a type of customer insight. Whom can you expect to convince? Who is worth reaching? (See *Chapter 7* for more on this.)

So, in this way, channels should be used in a trickle-down manner based on cost. No one has one favourite channel. Most people use many channels.

THE NEW CHANNELS

Throughout this book, we'll often mention the Google and Facebook (Meta) ecosystems when referring to paid media and advertising. We realize that these are not the only advertising platforms and that brands are certainly driving value from advertising across other platforms – including TikTok and retail media. From a personalization perspective, what matters is whether or not you as a marketer have the option of efficiently targeting specific audiences and can thus use these channels as an integrated part of the personalized customer experience. If this is not possible, then they can still be part of an interesting and effective marketing mix – it will just be harder to do any meaningful personalization.

THE POWER OF REPETITION

A term used in advertising is **effective frequency**.[2] This is a measure of how many times a person must be exposed to a classic (i.e. unpersonalized) advertising message before they respond and before further exposure is considered wasteful. It also applies to personalized communication – regardless of channel. Though some formats and channels spur greater attention and engagement, generally speaking it makes sense to repeat a message for a customer several times in order to increase the chances of it sinking in.

In advertising, this can be achieved through a very simple re-exposure of exactly the same advert. In email marketing, a reminder seemingly identical to the first message is generally considered acceptable by consumers – perhaps wrapped up slightly differently in terms of the subject line or introductory text (marketing copywriting – or simply 'copy'). If, for instance, it carries great importance for your results that your customers download and register on your app, it is definitely worth repeating a request to do so. In fact, this request could be included as a secondary message across email campaigns in general until the audience have taken the action. Consider, however, that not all customers will be interested in doing this, so some kind of expiration policy should be considered.

When you do identify a need to repeat an important message, you might also consider using multiple ways of saying the same thing. In this way, your message will stand a higher chance of being noticed and your brand will be considered more human and less mechanistically repetitive.

INSIGHTS COME FROM DATA

It is no secret that data plays a central role in personalization, namely in defining the insights. Sometimes a specific data point carries such great meaning or intent that it constitutes an insight in itself. If, for instance, you have behavioural data showing that a customer is browsing your web pages about how to cancel a subscription, naturally this is an insight that should not be missed. However, most insights go deeper and data exists in many forms.

Data can either be general and anonymous or relate to individual customers, and it can come from both qualitative and quantitative sources. Among advertising agencies, the term 'insight' has long been used to shape and justify campaigns. This type of insight rarely comes from first-party customer data. Rather, it more often comes from qualitative studies – based on focus groups, interviews, anthropological observations, and so on – combined with anonymized statistical data sources. This doesn't mean that these insights aren't valid or that they can't be used for personalization. In the case of media buying, it makes great sense to limit ad spending and focus on certain segments based on the data and segmentation criteria available in the Google and Facebook ecosystems. Explicit personalization, on the other hand, requires that you have specific customer data for each individual.

QUANTITATIVE DATA DRIVES INSIGHT; QUALITATIVE DATA DRIVES MESSAGING

Whereas quantitative data is the primary source of the insights used in personalization, qualitative data – and especially the interpretation thereof – can mean a lot for how a certain message is creatively crafted. For instance, consider the reactivation message for health club members at the start of this chapter. Qualitative data and insights will be useful in deciding what it is that could motivate a certain customer segment to perform a specific desired action. For example, why do the elderly members of PureGym generally go to the gym? The answer will mean a lot in terms of what the reactivation message should sound like.

Qualitative insights also matter a great deal for how both value propositions and platforms such as apps and websites are generally put together. Often qualitative insights will serve as inputs for how so-called personas are created. These personas take the form of narratives and serve as embodiments of specific important segments. The narratives help project participants to put themselves in the mind of the intended users – and thus design a service according to what the personas and not the designers themselves deem important.

ALL MODELS ARE WRONG – BUT SOME ARE USEFUL!

The famous statistician George Box is often quoted as having said that all models are wrong, but some are useful. The meaning behind this aphorism is obviously that all models are approximations of reality and as such naturally fail to capture all of the complexity that real life entails. That doesn't mean that they aren't useful, however. So, depending on what your aim is and what decision you are looking to make, some models will make it easier for you to make up your mind and choose the optimal course of action. The Bowtie of Personalization is no exception to this rule. It is intended to help you and your colleagues better understand personalization as a term and thus collaborate more efficiently to create value through personalization.

As we shall explore in the following chapters, the emphasis on the individual corners of the Bowtie of Personalization changes from one marketing discipline to the next. We will discuss how the emphasis shifts when you are working with campaigns (*Chapter 9*), marketing automation (*Chapter 11*), and personalization on inbound platforms such as websites and apps (*Chapter 13*). It will become clear where to focus to optimize value creation for both customers and your company within these disciplines.

FROM BOWTIE TO PYRAMID – WHAT DOES GOOD LOOK LIKE?

It is one thing to understand what personalization is and how it is applied in different marketing disciplines. It is another thing to know which parts of personalization to implement and in which order. For each of the marketing disciplines discussed in *Chapters 9, 11,* and *13* (campaigns, marketing automation, and inbound platforms), we offer a set of maturity levels. For each maturity level, we offer details of the scope of the likely personalization efforts of a company operating at that level.

We will conclude this part of the book by gathering the three maturity levels for each discipline into what we call the Pyramid of Personalization (see *Chapter 14*). For now, we're mostly concerned with discussing the scope – the personalized communication you choose to implement and that eventually becomes part of the customer experience. We will refer to this as the **front end** of the pyramid throughout the rest of the book. This is the part that creates effectiveness, as we discussed in *Chapter 2*. In *Part IV* of the book we shall examine the **back end** of the pyramid in greater detail. What is it that supports the personalized customer experience from an organizational point of view? This is more about organizational efficiency – again, as introduced in *Chapter 2*.

Together, the front end and the back end form the full Pyramid of Personalization, which is a full maturity model for working profitably with personalization across marketing disciplines. The reason we describe the model as a pyramid is that the more sophisticated your work with personalization becomes, the more it is customer-centric and channel agnostic, and the more it supports long-term value creation – regardless of which discipline you're mainly working with.

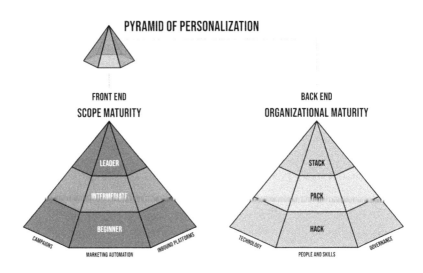

Figure 7. The front end and back end of the Pyramid of Personalization.

CHAPTER 7
INSIGHTS, PART 1: SEGMENTS

'How can we make our colleagues better understand that our customers have such different needs?' François-Yves ponders to himself. François-Yves works as Director of Marketing and Customer Strategy at the Canadian banking group Desjardins. Lately, he's been very occupied with the narrative power of personas and how these are built from customer segments. Personas are fictional characters who embody the central needs, desires, and traits of an organization's customers. Communicated through narratives, they make it easier for anyone to put their own bias aside and put themselves in the place of these people.

Desjardins has more than 7 million clients and offers services within personal banking, insurance, and wealth management – so where to start? Being a bank, it has been gathering customer data on both a profile and a behavioural level since day one. To understand its customers better, it has been doing deep work with data analytics to define the most significant segments within its customer database and how they are using the bank and its services. Desjardins now has a clear image of when clients generally buy their first car and their first home, when they become parents for the first time, and what that means for how they do business with the bank. They know how divorce or losing a family member can change people's lives and what this means for the bank too.

After combining this information with qualitative data from countless interviews, Desjardins is now at a place where it has better customer insight than ever. François-Yves knows that this insight will be a very valuable tool in the future. It will be useful not only in designing services but also in the way the bank designs campaign messaging. It will also make a substantial change to how Desjardins prioritizes its media spending. This will ultimately save large amounts of cash as well as increasing the odds of new clients ultimately becoming satisfied and profitable customers. 'Today is a good day,' François-Yves reflects!

The above narrative is a fictionalized account that captures the essence of how Desjardins works with segments. Segments make up the top corner of the Insights part of the Bowtie of Personalization. Note that when we refer to 'segments' in this book, we implicitly mean *customer* segments. As we touched upon in *Chapter 3*, segmentation is something you do to your customer database. The point is to divide it into smaller segments to enable you to manage more homogeneous groups of customers who will respond qualitatively differently from other segments to the content you choose to show them.

HOW ARE SEGMENTS BUILT?

Customer segments are fairly static groups of customers. Of course, people can change segments and even belong to multiple segments at the same time, so this is not an absolute truth. For example, the moment a child is born – or even the moment when a pregnancy test comes out positive – a person moves from one segment to another. As we shall discuss further in *Chapter 10*, this is referred to as a moment of truth.

Customer segments can be built using anonymous market insights. This is the method that strategic planners in advertising agencies tend to use. However, segments can also be built using advanced analytical models based on actual customer data.

The most classic marketing segments are often based on demographic information. If a customer has a specific gender, marital status, age, and kids, and lives in a certain neighbourhood, then they will most likely have more in common with people who share these characteristics than with other customers. Hence, these people can be treated somewhat similarly when it comes to marketing messaging and campaigns. However, this is not to say that this is necessarily exact knowledge and that it always applies. Keep in mind that segmentation on probabilistic, statistical, or even simple profile data is a very rough way of putting people in buckets and will not take into account any individual variations from the norm (which there certainly will be). So don't get too confident in your creative messaging when you address people from just one segment. Even if you do happen to have rather elaborate customer data, you still don't know who each individual is as a person and what's going on in their life, and thus how they will react to your message. Use segments to 'get it less wrong'.

Think back to the distinction between implicit and explicit personalization in *Chapter 3*. It is extremely important that if you are very explicit in addressing a certain circumstance or customer need, then this should be based on deterministic data – namely, data that has very little ambiguity and error margin and that you know belongs specifically to this very individual. Did they explicitly tell you that they were going through a divorce? If not, then tread carefully.

On the other hand, you might have defined a customer segment on deterministic data – for example, a customer having bought a specific car from your company. In this case, using this non-sensitive information explicitly will work better than addressing it implicitly.

SEGMENT BASED ON DETERMINISTIC DATA	+ SENSITIVE TOPIC	=	COMMUNICATE CAUTIOUSLY
SEGMENT BASED ON DETERMINISTIC DATA	+ NON-SENSITIVE TOPIC	=	COMMUNICATE CAUTIOUSLY
SEGMENT BASED ON PROBABILISTIC DATA	+ NON-SENSITIVE TOPIC	=	COMMUNICATE IMPLICITLY
SEGMENT BASED ON PROBABILISTIC DATA	+ SENSITIVE TOPIC	=	COMMUNICATE IMPLICITLY

TURNING SEGMENTS INTO PERSONAS

As in the Desjardins example, customer segments can be used to create more lively personas that people in your organization can relate to. This can make team members better at designing services and customer communications without being too biased and unknowingly designing for themselves instead. Within personalization, personas can certainly help as a kind of creative brief for putting together content with appropriate messaging, tone of voice, images, video, suggested products, and so on. When configuring marketing technology such as a CRM system or a marketing automation platform, however, there is more focus on the underlying criteria for when customers are considered to belong to a specific segment.

METHODS OF SEGMENTATION

Some of the most classic data used for segmentation is, of course, gender, age, and family patterns. There are many nuances to how gender is captured and interpreted, of course; however, people who identify as women and are of a particular age tend to be interested in different things than are people who identify as men of another age. And if they tell you that they have kids, then suddenly a whole new set of messages and offers could become relevant. Geographical location is naturally also a relevant data point – especially if your services vary based on place. Often this is referred to as localization.

ADVANCED SEGMENTATION – BEHAVIOURAL CLUSTERS

A very advanced way of working with segmentation is to have algorithms put together behavioural clusters dynamically. Within retail, this typically translates to 'people who buy certain products'. However, it could also mean 'people who watch certain shows' (Netflix), 'people who listen to these artists' (Spotify), or 'people who read certain articles' (FT.com).

These segments are rarely used manually or creatively as they are built dynamically, and even the number of desired segments can be dynamic. If, however, you took a manual look at the top five behavioural clusters in your company, there would be a fair chance that you'd be able to recognize those 'types of customer' and relate to who they are. And the outputs of algorithmic segmentation could even serve as inputs to the segments you choose to work with when your team is putting together creative messaging. In the case of Spotify and Netflix, these segments are put to use dynamically as the companies' content libraries are so immense and multifaceted. More on this when we cover the Content Feeds corner of the Bowtie of Personalization (see *Chapter 12*).

VALUE-BASED SEGMENTATION

Value-based segmentation entails dividing a customer database into segments based on how much money they currently spend with you – or their potential (i.e. how much money you predict they will spend with you).

Customers can be divided into value-based segments in many different ways. The most common split is probably into 'low spenders', 'medium spenders', and 'big spenders'. However, there is no universal definition of, for example, a 'big spender' so it is entirely up to you and your data analytics team to decide how to set the definitions. Data visualization can help greatly when determining how to define your segments and where to put the divisions. If, for instance, a visualization shows that there's a significant cluster of customers who spend between €800 and €1,000 per year with your business, another cluster of customers who spend between €200 and €400, and almost no customers in between, then perhaps one of the criteria for determining a 'big spender' could be set to having a spend of €800+ and not, for example, €350.

Another common value-based method of segmentation within transactional companies (such as retailers and travel agencies) is RFM segmentation. RFM stands for **recency, frequency, and monetary value**. A high score in recency would indicate that this customer segment has recently been shopping with you; a high score in frequency would indicate that they shop with you often; and a high monetary value would mean that they have spent a large sum with you – just like the 'big spenders'. A customer segment with a low recency score would make a good target for a win-back or 'we miss you' campaign, or even an automated flow. A segment consisting of customers with high frequency but low monetary value would make a good target for campaigns or flows aiming to increase customer lifetime value through cross-sales and/or aiming to drive customers' preference to products with a higher margin. Bear in mind that, in general, it is easier to get customers to come back and buy more of the same than it is to make them buy something completely different from you than they normally do.

Omnichannel retailers often divide customers into segments based on their shopping channel preferences: online, in-store only, and omnichannel. It is not uncommon to see a strong correlation between higher spend and an omnichannel shopping pattern. In terms of reporting, it is best practice to track how the size of the segments based on shopping-channel behaviour evolve over time. In terms of how you use this information, you might start by looking at relative segment values. For example, an omnichannel customer might be worth 40% more than the average single-channel customer (with single-purchase customers not taken into account). You might then look to increase the number of your omnichannel customers – for example, through targeted campaigns that offer channel-specific vouchers to single-channel shoppers for use in the channels they currently don't shop through.

USING VALUE-BASED SEGMENTS TO OPTIMIZE PAID MEDIA SPEND

Most advertising platforms (including Google and Facebook) offer the opportunity to map your existing segments onto corresponding audiences. So, apart from the value of using value-based segments in your reporting, they are also good for deciding which channels to use when you want your message to get attention. Obviously, you should consider the price per contact and thus you will most likely prioritize owned media over paid media (see *Chapter 6*). First of all, if you can get your message through and get the desired effect by sending emails and notifications alone, why bother exposing people to paid adverts? And for the customers who still haven't taken the desired action, consider showing ads only to segments with large potential (and be especially careful of using expensive telemarketing or direct mail).

Once you have decided which of your segments are high potential and thus worth exposing to ads, you should also consider using the 'similar audiences' (Google) or 'lookalike audiences' (Facebook) tools. The goal is for the advertising platforms' algorithms to find so-called behavioural twins of the segments that you are considering turning into paid media audiences. If you have good and plentiful first-party data, there is a high chance that these 'behavioural twin audiences' will become better customers in the future than the average new customer.

It should be pretty obvious from the above that segments can and should mean a lot when you are deciding on your creative messages, especially for campaigns. In the next chapter, we'll explore these messages more closely.

CHAPTER 8
CONTENT, PART 1: MESSAGES

'We need to position "Sweaty Sunday" differently from our key segments,' Jesper said. He was briefing the marketing team for SPORTMASTER's new club membership advantage. Once every quarter, members would receive a 25% discount on almost the full inventory. Of course, the big discount drew a lot of attention and to some extent drove a significant proportion of the company's sales. However, through his years-long experience, Jesper knew that there was an additional uplift to be had. SPORTMASTER's most valuable segment was family/child – namely, families with kids that do a lot of sports. Football was big with them – but these kids did a lot of different sports and there was no knowing what would be on the agenda this school term. In second and third place they had women and men without kids. These segments tended to be more fashion oriented and the dominant sports in the shopping behaviours of both segments were fitness and running.

The way SPORTMASTER addressed Sweaty Sunday – ranging across text, images, and the products the team chose to showcase in emails – should be totally different from one segment to the next. Jesper knew from experience that this could give them up to twice the sales that they'd otherwise get. Obviously, they had more segments than this, but Jesper also knew that the extra effect from additional content variants would quickly wane as they went further down the list of segments. For the rest of the segments they were better off doing more generic content. He'd make sure the customer club data and insights were used not only in emails and on the web but also in paid advertising. Existing

86

club members would see ads for Sweaty Sunday, and the Facebook and Google algorithms were set up to look for similar audiences to those they'd show ads to about signing up for membership and not missing the Sweaty Sunday discount. On Sunday afternoon, club members who had shown interest but hadn't yet made a purchase would receive a text message to further increase sales. Jesper felt confident that SPORTMASTER would meet its quarterly sales targets with this personalized cross-channel campaign.

The narrative above tells a story about how the sporting goods retailer SPORTMASTER leverages its creative messaging. The brand acknowledges the fact that when this messaging matches the corresponding segments, it drives higher sales and conversions. The team puts creative thought and energy into crafting messages that make it as obvious as possible for recipients that a specific message is relevant to them.

WHAT IS A MESSAGE?

A message is something you as a marketer have a need and desire to tell a recipient. As shown in *Chapter 4* – which explores why personalization works – it is clear that if you better match the message to the fundamental motives and preferences of each recipient, there will be much better recall and thus interest among those recipients.

Most messages will be about encouraging or enabling the recipient to *feel*, *know*, or *do* something that will be in your interest. For example, if you want them to feel more warmly about your brand, you'll humbly apologize for any mistakes made or show them content about your sustainability efforts and how you're fighting to create a greener future for all. If you want them to avoid wasted store visits, you'll show them that their local store is closed this upcoming Saturday due to maintenance. Or if the expiry date of their credit card is approaching, you'll ask them to update you with their new credit card details to avoid inconvenient service interruptions. In the case of our opening case study, SPORTMASTER sent its members the message that Sweaty Sunday was approaching.

VARIATIONS FROM CHANNEL TO CHANNEL

Following the Bowtie of Personalization, personalization is something that should happen before your message is built into a channel. So, ideally, you'll decide on whom to reach with which messages before creating channel-specific variants of each message. Depending on the channel, you'll have different options for text, images, video, and creative elements in general. But ultimately it will be the same message regardless of channel.

If you're working with a message about renewing an expiring subscription, then this will appear as a fairly short line of text in an SMS message and in a push notification to an app – or as a website notification if the recipient is logged in. The email version will have a subject line similar to that of the SMS message but with more elaborate text, images, and links in the body. The version used in targeted advertising would be a more subtle and implicit version of the same message. The right software can help you greatly in managing your key messages and insights centrally, and furthermore can make reporting easier across channels.

ADAPTING MESSAGE VARIANTS FOR DIFFERENT SEGMENTS

In the opening case study of this chapter, SPORTMASTER had different variants of the 'Sweaty Sunday' message for each of its customer segments. For the family/child segment, the team would use images of parents with kids and say directly in the text that 'if you're looking for kids' sports equipment, then now's the time'. They'd also highlight products that match this segment – more about that in *Chapter 12*.

As we learned in the previous chapter, customer segments can represent different geographies, religions, political standpoints, ethnic groups, and other demographics that you may consider when creating message variants. Major geographical differences in your customer database – such as northern versus southern hemisphere – could make you consider something as practical as whether or not to show snow in your Christmas greetings. Taking this further than geographical location means accommodating different religions and customs. Either you make sure you know who celebrates Christmas or you water the message down and send 'Season's greetings' instead of 'Merry Christmas'.

USING CULTURAL DIFFERENCES IN MESSAGE VARIANTS

Consider cultural differences in your message variants as well. How you greet a customer in, for example, the USA and Japan will be culturally very different. No one would be alarmed by the informal 'Hi Josh' in the USA, but a more formal 'Dear Mr Murakami' would be appropriate in Japan.

Cultural differences among your recipients can also matter greatly when it comes the images you use. When a company known to the authors launched in Russia, for instance, the locals were puzzled by the tattooed black woman on the front page of the company's website, especially given the connotations that tattoos have within Russia. There are very few black people in Russia and tattoos are heavily associated with the mafia. So, if the goal was to signal diversity and acceptance, then this was lost with an image having so many confusing local connotations.[1]

BEWARE OF POOR TRANSLATIONS

An important thing to be aware of when crafting local-language versions of messages is the difference between translation and localization. Direct translations can be at best hilarious and at worst damaging to a brand's image. In what now seems like ancient times, American Airlines wanted to promote the luxury of leather seats in its airplanes with the motto 'Fly in leather'. Directly translated into Spanish, this became 'Vuelo in cuero', which sadly had the ambiguous meaning of 'Fly naked'.[2] Motorola has used the slogan 'Hello Moto' for several years.[3] In Punjabi, however, 'Motto' is a common nickname used for obese people. How about launching a global campaign that potentially insults 23.5% of India's population?[4] Make sure that local markets are heard when launching localized content.

USING PARAMETRIZATION FOR EXTRA PERSONALIZATION

Using parameters or placeholders to dynamically insert data into messages on owned media (such as emails or websites) not surprisingly makes them feel more personal. For example, if you could see (on a website or via email) full usage insights on your company's subscription to a news service (e.g. FT.com), this would definitely feel personalized.

There are exceptions to the positive effects of parametrization, of course. For instance, we've all been tricked into thinking an email was specifically for us by the use of 'Hello $FirstName' personalization and then found that the rest of the email was totally not personalized. Consumers are smart – don't try and trick them into giving you higher open rates without delivering real value.

CREATING VALUE FOR CUSTOMERS IN YOUR MESSAGES

According to our definition of personalization, the goal is to create immediate and future business value. In order to create future business value for your company, it is important to also ensure that recipients of the messages you personalize perceive value. If you consistently don't and are perceived as too spammy because you send irrelevant messages, then you'll greatly jeopardize your future business value.

So, what, then, is 'value for the customer'? First of all, value can be either **gain oriented** or **pain oriented**. Going back to the fundamental motives framework (see *Chapter 4*), recipients will be strongly motivated by the idea of evading physical harm or disease, or even just economic loss, for themselves or their loved ones. In fact, these pain-oriented incentives are stronger than gain-oriented incentives.

CATEGORY ENTRY POINTS

Within advertising, famous adman Byron Sharp and his team at the Ehrenberg-Bass Institute for Marketing Science have coined the term 'category entry points' (CEPs).[5] These relate to situations where a consumer is thinking about your product and thus potentially 'entering into a buying decision' within the product category. If you're selling Coca-Cola, then the CEPs will include organizing a kid's party, buying drink mixers for a party, and so on. If you manage to make your brand top of mind (i.e. people think of your brand in these scenarios) and available (i.e. on the shelves in people's favourite grocery store) in these CEPs, then you will be doing well.

'CEP' is, of course, a branding term but it is still useful when you're working with personalization because it helps you craft the message related to the context in which a product can create value. As we shall later see, a CEP is also similar to what we call a 'moment of truth' within personalization.

VALUE CREATION IN A BROADER PERSPECTIVE

Value creation naturally has more depth than finding the perfect mixer for a cocktail party. If, for instance, you work at a charity such as the Red Cross, what then is the value you create for your donors? Are you delivering good conscience? Social capital? Or a physical product? It can easily become complex.

To help put value creation into perspective, we can consider the work of Forrester Research, as presented at the company's annual customer experience conference in 2022.[6] According to Forrester Research, value for customers is created in a value network, and this has great implications for how you conceptualize and communicate value. Value can be of an economic, functional, experiential, or even symbolic nature (see *Figure 8*).

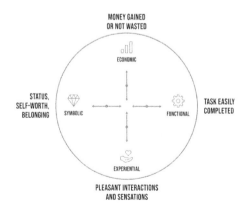

Figure 8. Forrester Research's four value dimensions.

Economic value might be provided through low prices, a discount, or a voucher. Functional value might be provided via usage tips, support, or even help performing a DIY task. Experiential value will be achieved through the actual use of a product or some sort of sensory allure, such as taste or feeling great. Symbolic value might come from knowledge that increases a person's social standing or self-affirmation. Consider, for instance, the value of storytelling about expensive products such as wine or art. Being able to tell a story about your new piece of jewellery or a particular Barolo wine is half the pleasure and makes you stand out in front of your friends. Symbolic value can also just come from the feeling of belonging to a group or the very personal and private feeling of having supported a good cause.

Considering all these different forms of value opens up many new messages you could consider. Personally, we are disappointed not to have seen automated follow-up emails about wine we recently purchased. How come we haven't seen any wine merchants helping us to tell good stories after a transaction has been made?

USING MESSAGE VARIANTS WHEN REPEATING A MESSAGE

Even if your intention in sending a message to customers is to have them experience value, it isn't necessarily a given that they will do what you propose. Just like in real life, within marketing you often have to repeat yourself quite a few times to get the response you're after. However, it can easily seem shallow if you constantly ask the same thing in the exact same manner. If, for instance, you are asking customers to download and use your app, then consider having variants of the message that make the request in different ways each time. This will make customers more likely to notice your message and thus increase your chances of success. Try different approaches and reasons for downloading the app, such as 'get notified of flash sales and offers' or 'try virtual make-up through our app' – same message, different argumentation.

FOCUSING ON MESSAGES WHEN WORKING OUTBOUND

As you've probably noticed, in marketing there's no time to wait around for people to notice your company and your offerings. Competitors would quickly steal the attention of your customers and you'd never increase your market share (or get any market share at all). Unless, of course, your product is the best thing since sliced bread – which others may still not notice that it is. Obviously, there is a lot you can do to increase your market share with inbound marketing, such as search engine optimization and search engine marketing. The difference is that customers need some kind of pre-existing intent in order to look for your company on search engines. So, if you want to maximize your success, you will need to use outbound communication – specifically, show customers adverts, and send them emails, text messages, and app notifications.

Reaching out to people who don't already have some sort of intent means that you're basically interrupting them or even disturbing them. A customer wants to watch a guitar lesson on YouTube and has to spend at least five seconds watching a preroll video from your brand. Another is looking through their inbox for a concert ticket and sees six newsletters at the top. A third is on their bike to work and suddenly their phone vibrates – it could be their friend, so they stop. Instead, it's a text message about the flash sales you're throwing.

Needless to say, in these situations it's extremely important to be on point. Customers are busy doing other things. You don't 'control their customer journey' – instead, you're intruding into their busy lives trying to get their attention. So you'd better earn their trust or they will switch you off. That's why personalization in outbound communication can make a huge difference.

IS IT REALLY FOR ME?

The grand old man of direct mail was Siegfried Vögele (1930–2014), a German who developed the dialogue method in the 1970s.[7] According to Vögele, people subconsciously ask themselves several questions when faced with direct mail: Who is it from? Is it really for me? Is it worth my time? For every question there needs to be a little 'Yes' in order for the recipient to proceed to the next question and hopefully arrive at the final big 'Yes' to whatever you propose in the direct mail.

When a person receives an envelope, they spend the first eight seconds reading the address, identifying the sender, and examining any other information. Then they may open it and unfold the content. All the while they are trying to find answers to those questions: Who is it from? Is it really for me? Is it worth my time? With emails, the process is much the same, although the attention span is far shorter than eight seconds. If you don't get customers' attention right there in the inbox overview, it doesn't matter how great your copy is within the email or which products you choose to put in there. Once your customer does open the email, though, the content within it had better be relevant as well. According to Statista.com, in 2021 consumers spent on average ten seconds reading those emails that they actually did open.[8] If it's not relevant, customers are quickly on to the next thing.

The same goes for all outbound performance marketing. If you're not hyper-relevant, you won't get the 'Yes' that you're after. And too many 'Nos' over time can lead to the 'Big No', with customers unsubscribing, turning off notifications, uninstalling your app, or simply ignoring your business.

So, when we compare the importance of messages with that of content feeds in the Bowtie of Personalization, it's clear that messages are what matter the most when working with outbound communication. Content feeds, on the other hand, are most important when working with inbound communication, where you already have the intent or the attention of the customer.

PERSONALIZING THE CHOICE OF COMMUNICATION CHANNEL

We discuss a lot of digital channels in this book, and for good reason. However, there are other channels – ones with less or no digital aspect – where the message can mean a lot. The most important person-to-person touchpoints are when your organization meets customers in your chat, your support centre, or in-store. In these cases, messages can mean a lot as well. We're not arguing that you should ask people to check out your current deals when they have just called you with a question. But once that question has been answered, you have a golden opportunity to ask a question of your own – to deliver one message.

So, what should that be? In the exact same way that you need different versions of your message for different digital channels, you need a 'talk script' version of each message for use by sales associates and call centre agents. According to Stefan Kirkedal, Head of Customer Insights, Loyalty and Media at Matas, the first seed in the success of the Danish health and beauty retailer Matas was to more systematically and persistently ask in-store customers whether they wanted to sign up to the company's loyalty scheme. Back then (in 2010) it wasn't proven that this would be more profitable than asking customers to add a small extra product to their purchase. It was a long-term bet, but it certainly paid off.

CHAPTER 9
PERSONALIZATION IN CAMPAIGNS

Throughout the discussion of segments and messages in the previous two chapters, there has been an almost unavoidable undertone around working with campaigns – and for good reason. It's time to draw our first set of conclusions on what matters the most within personalization in the major marketing disciplines – in this case, campaigns. In this chapter we'll define the term 'campaign' and draw conclusions about how personalization is used to optimize campaigns and what kind of value creation you can expect. This is all about tying together the upper part of the Bowtie of Personalization, as *Figure 9* shows.

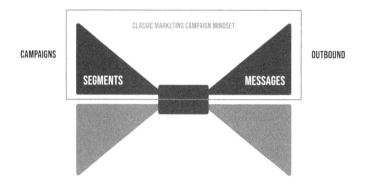

Figure 9. The top of the Bowtie of Personalization captures the essence of working with personalization in campaigns.

DEFINING THE TERM 'CAMPAIGN'

All these definitions – are they really necessary? Doesn't everybody know what a campaign is? Well, yes and no. In this book we follow the distinction between campaigns and customer lifecycle communication (CLC) as introduced in Rasmus Houlind and Colin Shearer's book *Make It All About Me* (see *Figure 10*).[1]

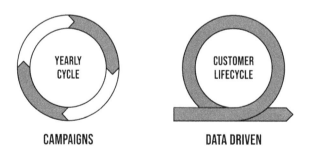

Figure 10. How campaigns diverge from data-driven customer lifecycle communication.

The book says:

For many companies, marketing campaigns follow the production cycle. And quite often the production cycle follows the four seasons. This is not wrong, and it does help to increase relevance that autumn-related products are marketed in the autumn. On top of the seasonal track, you'll have the yearly blockbuster occasions, such as Valentine's Day, Mother's Day, Singles' Day (Asia), Black Friday and Christmas.

It continues:

These tactics are all company-centric and follow a campaign mindset. You know the date is coming and prepare the best campaign possible across paid and owned media. Hopefully you are using data where you have it to select the right audiences in paid media and to personalize the message to each customer in owned media.

In addition to seasonal campaigns and big blockbuster occasions, you probably have (and should have) one or several weekly newsletters – all depending on how frequently your customers tend to interact with your services or shop with you, of course. A grocery store's customers will interact frequently, a pension company's customers will interact infrequently. Since the send-out times for these communications will depend on the current date and time, we also define these as campaigns, albeit miniature versions.

CLC, on the other hand, is triggered by behavioural data (or potentially a lack of it) from your customers. We'll cover CLC and marketing automation in *Chapter 11*.

VALUE CREATION IN PERSONALIZED CAMPAIGNS

So how, then, is value created in personalized campaigns? First of all, the time span of campaigns is relatively short. The longest campaign period in many countries is probably the Christmas sales, which last for around a month or more. This period begins shortly after the effects of Black Friday and Cyber Monday have waned and lasts until Boxing Day or just after Christmas Day. Shortly after – or at best even within – a campaign period you'll know whether you're doing well and be able to see the return you're getting for the extra time and resources you have potentially invested in your personalization efforts.

Seasonal campaigns have been the default marketing tactic ever since Eve was selling apples in the Garden of Eden (it was an autumn campaign, by the way). The conclusion of a marketing campaign is the default time for evaluating its effects. As marketers, we are used to this fairly short time perspective when we are making up our minds on whether a campaign activity was good or bad. In contrast, the effects of CLC and marketing automation should be evaluated over a longer time perspective (again, this will be explored in *Chapter 11*).

Value creation for personalized campaigns comes in four categories, namely:

1. Increasing sales to prospects and customers
2. Increasing the efficiency of campaigns by reusing dynamic logic for content
3. Saving costs by optimizing ad spend and avoiding returned orders and dissatisfaction
4. Charging money from suppliers through retail media

INCREASING SALES TO PROSPECTS AND CUSTOMERS

When you are aiming to increase sales to prospects and customers by using personalization in campaigns, the lowest-hanging fruit is naturally to craft one creative message per major customer segment. This message should then be adopted for use in each communication channel. Let your creative team decide which of the classic marketing segments (see *Chapter 7*) will most likely respond best to personalized copy, tone of voice, images, etc. in your key message. You can also consider using value-based segments to personalize which price points of products to include or, in the case of charities, how much money to ask for in your plea.

With regard to paid media, there are several things you should consider doing. They all rely on your integration of customer segments built on first-party data into paid media ecosystems. A draft plan could look like this:

1. Increase your bid on paid media for high-potential customer segments and their behavioural twins (see Chapter 7) that the advertising platforms can identify
2. Match the creative messages shown in your advertising to the specific segments
3. Start display and paid social advertising a few days before turning to the more conversion-oriented search engine marketing and owned media (such as email, SMS, and app push)
4. Remember reminders for non-clickers and non-buyers – if your offer is especially good and/or time sensitive then consider using the more intrusive SMS or app push notifications for reminders

According to Jesper Holm Pedersen, Head of Loyalty at the Danish sporting goods retailer SPORTMASTER, the increase in top-line sales from the above personalization tactic for a campaign can easily be as high as 100%. They also see click rates tripling and sales doubling when campaigns are handled in this manner. Expect 30–50% of this effect to come from the personalization of content to different segments and the remaining part from intelligent orchestration across channels.[2]

According to Dorte Karlsson, previous Head of Data & Insights at the media company Storyhouse Egmont, they saw a cost-per-acquisition of 30% of normal spend when they prioritized advertising for previous subscribers, thus leaving more budget to chase totally new customers. Your previous customers could very well be your high-potential prospects.[3]

Keep in mind that there will be diminishing returns from additional creative versions for each segment. If you have so many variants that they start to look alike, then it's probably not worth it.

INCREASING THE EFFICIENCY OF CAMPAIGNS BY REUSING DYNAMIC LOGIC FOR CONTENT

During the 2022 Winter Olympics, Warner Bros. Discovery optimized the content of emails to fans in many different ways. Dynamic blocks of content were put together by feeding relevant content based on the recipients' preferences.

Using data on the previous behaviours of each recipient, different leaderboards were shown to each individual containing the teams and sports the algorithm believed were most relevant to them. The send-out logic and the segment was the same – but the content within the email was dynamic. For a specific dynamic block of content, which dynamically put together the medals table for each recipient based on their nationality, there was a saving of 75% in production time.[4]

SAVING COSTS BY OPTIMIZING AD SPEND AND AVOIDING RETURNED ORDERS AND DISSATISFACTION

Obviously, cost savings aren't the primary goal of a campaign. However, you can also use personalization tactics to save money on campaigns – or at least save yourself from unnecessary costs and trouble.

The first personalization trick to pull in this regard is to exclude existing subscribers or 'customers who have recently purchased' from an upcoming campaign. This is done, once again, by sharing customer segments built on first-party data with the paid media advertising networks – this time configuring them to exclude said segments from all paid acquisition marketing.

Needless to say, customers who already have a health club subscription won't buy a second one – and customers who have just bought clothes at full price need not be made aware of the fact that you are now offering 20% off. Should they receive such a communication, the chances are that they will return the item they have just purchased and buy it again with the discount. That will leave you with all the handling costs and most likely the customer will still be irritated.

You could also consider excluding low-potential customers while you're at it. Why waste perfectly good advertising budget on customers who most likely won't buy anything? You can identify your low-potential segments either through predictive algorithms or using third-party data, for example through statistical enrichment services such as Geomatic or Mosaic.[5]

At the other end of the spectrum, you can also experiment by excluding customers from your paid media who have such high potential and loyalty that you believe they'll convert anyway. Or you might at least delay the adverts until you've seen who will convert using your owned media.

In the exact same way that you can hone your effectiveness when choosing between paid and owned media, you can also choose between any media with varying costs per communication. Prioritize customer segments centrally and apply the more expensive channels (such as SMS, telemarketing, and direct mail) for the remaining customers that you still believe it's worth reaching.

The amount that can be saved in this way of working with personalization will vary greatly from company to company. For subscription-based companies, though, it should almost be considered a crime not to exclude existing customers.

According to Mads Jefsen, Marketing Director at the Danish football club F.C. Copenhagen (FCK), they work deliberately with first-party data in their paid advertising. For instance, they exclude all season ticket and subscription holders from acquisition ads on paid media. Their advertising tool has an approximate figure for how large FCK's potential ticket-buying audience is. Depending on the parameters set in the tool, this audience could be larger or smaller. However, if it for example were in the region of 200,000 people, then excluding 20,000 people through first-party data could potentially save the club 10% of its media spend.

CHARGING SUPPLIERS MONEY THROUGH RETAIL MEDIA

Retail media could easily make up a whole book on its own. We chose to include it here as it is definitely a tactic that involves personalization and where first-party data insights are used to show specific content to select customers. The difference is that this time the company gets money for doing this, not only through sales but also from suppliers in the form of fees.

We refer to it here as 'retail media' even though any sector with suppliers and sponsors could potentially make money this way. The major players within retail media are naturally Amazon and eBay, but within the more traditional retail space you'll see frontrunners such as Best Buy and Walmart in the USA, and Carrefour and Tesco leading the European market. Outside retail, you'll see online grocery delivery platform Instacart raising the bar, but payment services such as Afterpay and Klarna are also looking into this.

The mechanism of retail media is basically to take payment for exposing select customers to highlighted products and offers from suppliers. This is done either by showing these products and offers on owned media (website, in-app, email) or simply by advertising on behalf of the suppliers. On your inbound platforms, there can be room for both offers and promotions in top-line banners, and products can be highlighted in your content feeds. So-called **category captainship** will put the supplier's product in a sponsored placement on top of, but in line with, the remaining inventory (in much the same way as paid ads used to take up only the two top places in a Google Search result page).

If you are actually selling the advertised product, this is referred to as **endemic advertising** – if not, then it's called **non-endemic advertising**. As an example of non-endemic advertising, imagine that you sell barbecue sauce but not barbecue grills. You might then take money from Weber (for example) to advertise Weber grills to the people you know recently bought barbecue sauce. Non-endemic advertising requires specific consent under most jurisdictions.

The reason that retail media is interesting for suppliers is principally that many of them, and especially fast-moving consumer goods (FMCG) producers, have very little access to first-party data (such as transactions). Their resellers (in this case, potentially, you) stand a much better chance of knowing who exactly is buying the supplier's products and who is buying the competitors' – and could thus be up for trying something different. So, for instance, Heinz could buy a special retail media campaign through Tesco for barbecue sauce targeting people who previously (but not too recently) bought a competing brand of barbecue sauce. A good offer there could help Heinz to win market share. A second reason that retail media is interesting for suppliers is that we are seeing a great decline in the availability of third-party data due to the death of cookies and data deprecation. As a result, traditional marketing tactics for FMCG producers are becoming less attractive.

In a market where margins are under pressure, retail media can make up a very interesting new revenue stream. According to Terence Kawaja from LUMA Partners, margins can be as low as 2% on groceries but as high as 40% on retail media (presumably when you are selling your own digital real estate).[6] Retailers we have spoken with on the topic suggest that the margins may be even higher, since the only cost is the labour needed for selling the digital property and running the campaigns. The volume, of course, is very small compared to the core business.

Retail media is new territory for most retailers, and the technology and processes needed to support it are currently not very mature. The area is especially complex for retailers that also sell their own private-label products. Tesco, for instance, needs to make decisions at scale about whether it is more profitable to put its own barbecue sauce in first place (based on that product's margin) versus putting the sponsored Heinz barbecue sauce in first place (with a smaller margin, but plus the media fee and then minus the potential loss of goodwill from customers). How should the company potentially sell such a placement efficiently and subsequently sort its products across zillions of product feeds to maximize their margins? And how should the company report the effects back to the supplier? These are new questions that companies selling retail media to suppliers need to address.

The effect of retail media from a supplier perspective can be measured with much higher accountability than is possible for most other media purchases such companies make. This is mostly a good thing for the suppliers, but it also has some bad connotations. It is good because, in the example above, the *direct sales* of the Heinz barbecue sauce can be measured on Tesco.com and reported back to the supplier. However, it is bad because this is not normally how FMCG producers measure the effect of their media spend. How do they then compare and integrate this into their existing reporting structures? In the end, however, it is likely to be very attractive indeed for FMCG producers to market their product right there and then in the moment of truth when the customer is shopping for a barbecue party on the retailer's ecommerce site.

As of now, retail media is still in its infancy. This means that FMCG producers are still buying retail media from a campaign perspective – as in 'Let's do a barbecue campaign in the two weeks leading up to Summer

Break and the following four weeks'. They are mainly following the yearly cycle and the four seasons. This is why we chose to include this tactic in the chapter on campaigns.

In the future, however, as retail media matures, it will also be bought and sold more as an 'always on' service. For example, imagine cosmetics brands paying retailers to always send a rich storytelling message with advice for usage and further product inspiration from their universe the first time a consumer buys a product of theirs. This is more in line with CLC and marketing automation.

MATURITY LEVELS FOR PERSONALIZED CAMPAIGNS

Combining insights-based customer segments with the right messages is not anywhere near going out of style. Even though there is a movement towards a more 'always on' way of working with marketing automation, there will still be good business to be made by marketing to customers based on the yearly cycle, the four seasons, and the blockbuster occasions with a personalized offer to boost conversions and maximize sales. In this chapter, we have shown how to maximize profit by increasing the top line through personalization, how to optimize media spend and potentially even save money through personalization, and lastly how to start tapping the potential of retail media and get paid by suppliers to run campaigns on their behalf.

Working with personalization in campaigns is an area you can continue to become better at. In the table below we have conceptualized three archetypical maturity levels for how you personalize your campaigns. You can use this table to get an idea of your approximate maturity level as well as a suggested scope for further development.

PYRAMID OF PERSONALIZATION - FRONT END

SCOPE MATURITY

CAMPAIGNS

LEADER

AI-BASED CALCULATION OF SEGMENTS ON ALL DATA TYPES
AI-BASED MATCH OF SEGMENTS WITH MESSAGES
LIFECYCLE MESSAGES AND 'CALLS TO ACTION' INCLUDED IN CAMPAIGNS
CHANNEL-AGNOSTIC CONTENT PRODUCTION
CHANNEL-AGNOSTIC PERSONALIZATION LOGIC
WIDE REUSE OF EXECUTION LOGIC WITH BUILT-IN SUPPRESSION PRINCIPLES
MOST SEASONAL CAMPAIGNS AUTOMATED
CAMPAIGNS SPAN MULTIPLE OWNED AND PAID CHANNELS

INTERMEDIATE

AUTOMATED EXCLUSIONS IN PAID MEDIA
SIMPLE RULE-BASED SUPPRESSION LOGIC IN USE
REUSE OF SEGMENTATION AND CAMPAIGN EXECUTION LOGIC
RULE-BASED SEGMENTATION ACROSS DATA TYPES
DEMOGRAPHIC AND VALUE-BASED SEGMENTATION IN USE
CAMPAIGNS SPAN MULTIPLE OWNED CHANNELS WITH MULTIPLE STEPS

BEGINNER

MANUAL REPRODUCTION OF SEGMENTATION, CONTENT, AND EXECUTION LOGIC
MANUAL EXCLUSIONS IN PAID MEDIA
SIMPLE SEGMENTATION ON ZERO-PARTY DATA
SIMPLE 'HELLO $FIRSTNAME' PARAMETRIZATION OF OTHERWISE GENERIC EMAILS
PRIMARY MESSAGES ARE SIMPLE OFFERS AND DISCOUNTS
CONTENT LIVES IN-CHANNEL
SEPARATE EMAILS PER MESSAGE VARIANT

CHAPTER 10
INSIGHTS, PART 2: MOMENTS OF TRUTH

Marie knew this wasn't the best solution. The results, however, were still quite good, which confirmed her suspicion that her team was onto something even better. The FT.com subscribers who'd received the usage digest before year's end and had been confronted with their actual use of FT.com – how often they'd used the service, how many articles they'd read, and even how many articles they'd shared with friends – showed a significantly lower churn than the control group, to whom the team had chosen not to send the digest. This was good, of course. However, Marie knew that although a lot of subscriptions were up for renewal around new year, the majority were scattered throughout the year. So why not use this insight and trigger these usage digests on an individual level in accordance with the individual renewal dates?

She went through the idea with her team and they all agreed, plus they came up with additional ideas. Josh suggested they combine the usage insights with the algorithmically determined subscriber-specific price sensitivity insights to determine whether to tease for an upsell to the next tier. Brilliant! Nathalie suggested they expand on the flow and look to see whether there were more than five individual subscribers within each customer's company. If this was the case, then they could automatically set up a task for their account managers in customer relationship management (CRM) to reach out and discuss the option of a group subscription with the client. It wouldn't be the easiest thing in the world to set up – but once they'd done so it would run automatically and continually improve their churn rates as well as customer lifetime value throughout the year. They should even see a lift in group subscriptions if Marie's suspicions held true. And they usually did.

WHAT IS A MOMENT OF TRUTH?

A moment of truth is one type of insight. It is much more dynamic than a customer belonging to any of the traditional marketing or value-based segments that we discussed in *Chapter 7*. A moment of truth is essentially a moment in time where a customer or potential customer is – or should be – making up their mind about a decision that involves your company. Should they go to the health club today even though they haven't been there for a while? Should they purchase the bikini? Should they put their loan payments on hold for the summer holiday? Should they go for a test drive in that car they have researched so much?

In the example above, Marie is trying to accentuate or even create the feeling among FT.com subscribers that they are getting a lot of value from their subscription. The timing is just before renewal so that when renewal comes around, hopefully the subscriber will recall this feeling and be more likely to renew. Marie is trying to create the intent of renewing the subscription – in an implicit and subtle way.

MOMENTS OF TRUTH BELONG TO THE CUSTOMER

In its essence, the moment of truth belongs to the customer – and not to your business – in much the same way that a customer's journey belongs to that individual customer. This is due to the fact that you basically have no way of knowing what goes on in the lives or heads of your customers. As *Chapter 7* explained, no matter how good you become at collecting and integrating data – and no matter how fine-tuned your algorithms are – you'll never get a full picture of what is going on with each customer. So, the best you can do is try to be less wrong.

Make approximations based on the data that you do have. Did someone leave an item in their basket on your website? It could mean that they were disturbed and really wanted to buy it! Or did they just want to see what the actual shipping costs were? Or did they accidentally add a product they don't really want? Or perhaps they are just waiting to see if you'll send them a discount voucher... Chances are that customers who leave stuff in their shopping basket will have a much higher interest in shopping with you – so of course you should try and make this happen.

As the popular and perhaps slightly naive saying about personalization goes, it's about sending the right message at the right time. If you get the moment of truth right, the right message could make the difference between the customer making the decision that is in your favour – or the opposite.

DISCOVERING VS CREATING INTENT

There's a difference, however, between whether you're trying to discover intent in your customers or create intent where there isn't necessarily any there to begin with. All outbound marketing is basically around creating intent.

An example that is often used when discussing how to discover intent is when behavioural data from a company's website shows that someone in the northern hemisphere is browsing for a bikini in February. This is a clear indication of intent! There is most likely a good reason for the behaviour since it's unlikely that there will be many casual browsers in this category at this time. Again, though, you can't know for sure what the reason for this behaviour is. Could it be that someone is browsing for a present? Or that they need a bikini to take on holiday to a warm destination? Or might they just like to wear bikinis at home...? Nonetheless, it is still a significant indication of intent. Not proof – but a strong indication that this customer has the intent to buy a bikini very soon, either from you or from somewhere else. If you deliver the right message right now or very soon, there's a chance you can affect the decision in your favour.

THE DANGER OF CREATING AN UNINTENDED INTENT

In the example from FT.com that we used to kick off this chapter, there isn't necessarily any apparent intent from the customers who receive the message. They could be either satisfied or dissatisfied. They could be either heavy users or light users. For some customers the message may serve the intended purpose – while for others it could serve as a reminder definitely *not* to renew their subscription.

If you have a good product that people generally use, it should not be difficult to decide whether to send out usage statistics like FT.com does. But still, some will see the message as a reminder to cancel their subscription when the time comes. That can leave you in a dilemma – should you still send it to everyone, or perhaps omit the ones who have light usage? It depends…

In *Chapter 3* we mentioned a conference presentation given by Gibson Biddle, former Vice President of Product at Netflix.[1] In the same presentation, Biddle shared this exact dilemma with the audience but with the choice of whether or not to send a payment reminder to trial customers before the first payment after the end of the free trial. Wasn't it the responsibility of the customer to only sign up for services they intended to use and also to leave before the trial ended and money was withdrawn? On paper, yes – and Biddle conceded that by not sending a reminder, Netflix would probably have to handle a fair number of complaints but at the same time gain a little more money from trial subscribers who weren't necessarily ideal customers anyway. However, Netflix chose to send the payment reminder to everyone, despite the cost. Yes, a few more people would have chosen to end their subscription, but the brand trust that this message built with existing customers was believed to generate much more future business value. This is a brilliant example of the potential trade-off between short-term and long-term business value.

If you find yourself in this dilemma and you suspect that your customers aren't using the service and will most likely choose to quit if reminded about an upcoming payment, then we'd argue that there is something wrong with your product. It is not acceptable to make up for this by falling back on dodgy or even downright unethical personalization tactics.

FINDING MOMENTS OF TRUTH

In contrast to the insight of segments, moments of truth are dynamic and fleeting by nature. As the fundamental motives framework suggests (see *Chapter 4*), any of the fundamental motives can be active or inactive at any time. So, a customer might ponder a certain decision over a long period of time, but this doesn't mean that they are constantly thinking about it. As a marketer it is your job to get them back into activating the fundamental motive that relates to your product or service. You're not trying to make them buy something they don't need – rather, you're trying to make them buy something they need before they'd otherwise do so, and to increase the chance that they will buy it from you and not from a competitor.

DYNAMIC DATA INDICATES A MOMENT OF TRUTH

The data clues you can collect and that will serve as indicators of moments of truth consist of behavioural data from websites, emails, apps, and digital sensors in products, in-store, and so on. For instance, behavioural data from a website would enable you to discover the customer who is looking for a bikini in February. Additionally, you can use data from trans-actions, products, subscriptions, and other details from the customer rela-tionship. In the example of FT.com, Marie used data from customers' subscriptions to individually trigger the emails.

Most countries have public registers and databases that can serve as third-party data. This could be, for example, real estate databases and licence plate registries. These can also be used to identify moments of truth. Knowing from a real estate database that a customer of your furniture business has moved to a bigger house, for instance, could signal to you that they'll be looking to buy more furniture soon.[2]

ABSENCE OF DATA CAN ALSO INDICATE A MOMENT OF TRUTH

In *Chapter 6*, when we introduced the Bowtie of Personalization, we used the example of PureGym DK reaching out to all of its members who hadn't been to the gym for a while. This is an example of using an absence of data to identify a moment of truth. For each member, PureGym would expect to see behavioural data from its clubs indicating attendance between one and five times per week. If it doesn't in fact see this data for a specific member over a period of two weeks (for example), then potentially the member could subconsciously be slipping out of the habit of going to the gym. Or have they been on holiday? Or have they been sick?

Again, this is not an exact science and there are many potential reasons for certain data to be there or not to be there. If you're not certain, then don't paint yourself into a corner where you claim to know what's going on. What PureGym knows is that there is no data coming from the clubs for a specific member, and they can do explicit personalization related to this knowledge. As for the potential reasons, they should tread carefully and not assume there's a habit being broken. Therefore, in a reactivation message, they should be curious and open as to what the reason for the absence could be, and gently suggest what the customer could do if a lack of motivation is indeed the cause.

Another example where a lack of data can indicate a moment of truth relates to win-back offers. If you don't have any transactional data showing that a customer has purchased from you over, say, the past three months, then there's a fair chance that indeed they haven't bought anything and that they may not do so again without a little extra carrot. A win-back offer or voucher could be the right message. *But* could it also be that your customer has lost their loyalty card and is still shopping with you? Or that they've forgotten their password for your app and can't be bothered to figure it out when purchasing? Or that they've bought something so small that they don't care about having it registered and earning the meagre number of loyalty points you give in return? Or that someone else from the same family has made a purchase for the household? Sometimes posing a question can be the best message, rather than assuming any one particular interpretation. If you're using email, include three options that the customer can simply click to let you know what's happening.

DIGGING DEEPER INTO MOMENTS OF TRUTH

We realize that the term 'moments of truth' is in use for many different purposes and with slightly different meanings. In the following, we'll dig a little deeper into this discussion.

HOW GOOGLE USES THE TERM 'MOMENT OF TRUTH'

Over the years, Google has used the term 'moment of truth' as well as the term 'micro-moments'. In 2011, Google criticized the use of the term FMOT (first moment of truth) by Procter & Gamble and coined its own term: ZMOT (zero moment of truth).[3] According to Google, the 'real' moment of truth (in all likelihood) happens way before the customer stands at the till and reaches for their credit card. Rather, it happens when the customer makes up their mind to make the purchase after having interacted with a plethora of channels digitally and in real life. This is the ZMOT and it could have been weeks earlier. In this book, we're expanding on the idea of the ZMOT to make it apply to all kinds of customer decisions that somehow involve your company.

In 2015, Google expanded on the topic of the ZMOT with a more holistic view of so-called micro-moments. The company defines micro-moments as follows:

Micro-moments occur when people reflexively turn to a device – increasingly a smartphone –to act on a need to learn something, do something, discover something, watch something, or buy something. They are intent-rich moments when decisions are made and preferences shaped.[4]

We do appreciate and agree with this more customer-journey-oriented perspective, but we disagree when it comes to the implicitness of intent. If you are making the most of your money from intent-based search marketing, then it makes sense. However, if as a marketer you always waited around until an intent was present, you'd be losing out. Hence our definition of moments of truth as times when a 'customer or potential customer is – or *should be* – making up their mind about a decision that involves your company'. You could almost say the purpose of an outbound message is to *make* the customer turn to a device (or store).

ALGORITHMIC INDICATIONS OF MOMENTS OF TRUTH – USING AI AND ADVANCED ANALYTICS

Returning once again to the PureGym DK example, we saw how the company used two weeks of absence from the gym to identify when they needed to reach out to members to make sure more people got back in the ring. This is a very simplistic way of determining an insight, but of course there are more advanced methods.

Within marketing, artificial intelligence (AI) was a big buzzword in 2018 and 2019, taking over from big data (2014/2015) and business intelligence (the Stone Age!). Business owners can use AI algorithms (self-learning or not) to determine churn propensities, brand affinity scores, or similar. A churn propensity could be represented as a score between 0 and 1 showing the likelihood of an individual customer cancelling their subscription. A brand affinity score would signify the degree to which a customer was fond of a particular brand. The scores and propensities are calculated based on various data inputs to an analytics model or algorithm, which then produces outputs (i.e. the scores and propensities) for marketers to act upon. In the case of the churn propensity score, the model might also provide underlying reasons so that marketers can motivate behaviour that (statistically speaking) will reduce the churn risk for each individual.

If you work with AI and analytical models to determine propensity scores and such, then keep in mind that this is not deterministic knowledge (see *Chapter 7*). As with any other moment of truth, you can't tell for sure what's going on or how 'correct' or precise the score is in each case. So, once again, use this probabilistic insight with caution – especially in terms of how explicitly (see *Chapter 3*) you are addressing the insights from it.

NOT ALL MOMENTS OF TRUTH ARE MARKETING'S RESPONSIBILITY

One important thing to keep in mind is that not all moments of truth belong to marketing. This is based on the idea that marketing does not necessarily own the part of the customer lifecycle where the customer relationship could benefit from a proactive outbound message. Often, moments of truth aren't related to direct short-term value creation but instead address soft topics such as uncertainty, gratitude, knowledge, and storytelling.

However, this shouldn't stop you from reaching out to customers when they have questions such as 'Are my goods on the way?', 'How is my claim handled?', 'Did you receive my return order?', 'How is my donation spent?', or 'What was the story behind this furniture design again?' A proactive message in these moments can greatly affect long-term value in terms of brand trust, customer lifetime value, net promoter score (see *Chapter 14*), and thus word of mouth.

MOMENTS OF TRUTH MATTER THE MOST WITHIN MARKETING AUTOMATION

In the book *Make It All About Me*, Rasmus Houlind and Colin Shearer point out and describe several classic moments of truth in a typical retail and subscription customer lifecycle.[5] They roughly divide the customer lifecycle into three phases: attract, grow, and retain. Within these three phases, they describe several suggested moments of truth to be addressed with automated communication on channels that fit each end customer's preferences (see *Figure 11*).

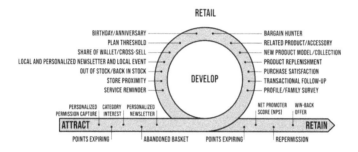

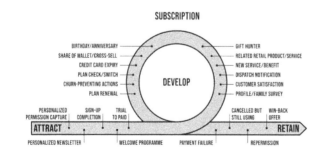

Figure 11. Examples of typical moments of truth in a retail and a subscription customer lifecycle. Source: *Make It All About Me*, Houlind & Shearer, 2019.

If you're short of ideas as to which moments of truth you could look for, then this is a great source of inspiration, especially if you're more used to thinking in a campaign mindset rather than organizing your ideas around marketing automation. Take a look at the ideas above to get your imagination going and start thinking beyond abandoned basket emails and triggered pleas to review the shopping experience on Trustpilot.

We discussed in *Chapter 9* how segment-based insights are what matter the most when you are working with your seasonal campaigns and need to decide which variants to develop for your creative messages. When it comes to working with marketing automation and customer lifecycle communication, however, you should instead focus on moments of truth. The number of important moments of truth you address with relevant messages matters far more than having these messages in variants for each segment. Value creation in marketing automation is the topic of our next chapter.

CHAPTER 11
PERSONALIZATION IN MARKETING AUTOMATION

Marketing automation (sometimes also called customer lifecycle communication) is a way of automatically communicating to customers the best possible message that matches the moment of truth you believe the customer to be in. Going back to the old personalization mantra of delivering 'the right message, at the right time, to the right person, in the right channel', automation touches on the first three parts – and, if we get our channel prioritization right, all four. This is in contrast to the campaign mindset (see *Chapter 9*), where we've already decided to reach out to one or several large customer segments and aren't too concerned about whether the timing is ideal for them. But hey – it's Thursday, and we promised to send weekly newsletters before the weekend, right?

Here, instead of looking solely at the upper part of the Bowtie of Personalization, we're now focusing on the portion from the bottom left, containing moments of truth, to the top right, containing messages (see *Figure 12*). More specifically, we're looking at the second core marketing discipline – marketing automation – and how to work across the Bowtie of Personalization.

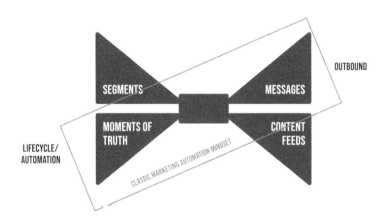

Figure 12. Marketing automation: matching moments of truth with messages that make a positive difference for the customer and your business.

VALUE CREATION IN MARKETING AUTOMATION

Getting the timing right for each individual carries perhaps the greatest opportunity to be perceived as relevant. And when it comes to getting people's attention, there's almost no better tactic for being perceived as relevant. Of course, since you'll never have a complete data picture and know exactly what's going on inside the heads of your customers, you'll always be playing a guessing game to some extent. So, once again, it's about optimizing relevance in a non-perfect world – realizing you won't get it right for everyone all the time.

SEGMENTS AND CONTENT FEEDS ARE SECONDARY IN MARKETING AUTOMATION

We discussed in earlier chapters how segments matter a lot when you are personalizing your messages in campaigns. For marketing automation, the majority of the value creation lies in getting the timing right and not so much in whether or not the message has multiple variants that are personalized for each segment. This doesn't mean that you shouldn't consider making multiple variants of your marketing automation messages – more that you should consider making and launching several automation flows before considering developing multiple variants of the content within these flows. Going back to the PureGym example (introduced in *Chapter 6*) around addressing inactivity in a health club member, it might be valuable to go from using a generic message to using a variant for each segment. However, you will get much greater value from sending a generic message than from sending none at all. So always consider whether your time is better spent developing more flows that address more moments of truth rather than making variants of existing ones.

The same goes for content feeds. It often makes sense to have product feeds in your outbound emails. If you have an email that goes out 40 minutes after a customer has abandoned their basket, then it could be a good idea to include the products they left behind in combination with other products that could be either substitutes for or complementary to the ones in the basket. There are many potential reasons for the customer not completing the purchase, so your product feeds could provide inspiration for customers where the exact products in the basket perhaps weren't the right ones. The main point, however, is that the most important thing about the abandoned basket email is that it exists and that it is being triggered. The rest you will have to test to see whether there is any substantial difference in the effect.

The actual contents of the abandoned basket and the additional products may add a modest amount of additional value. However, the key point is that the personalized timing alone will lead to substantial open, click, and conversion rates. So, in this case especially, don't let 'perfect' become the enemy of 'good'.

FOR MARKETING AUTOMATION, CONSIDER VALUE OVER THE LONG TERM

With marketing automation, you'll have a better chance of being perceived as relevant than if you send campaigns. However, you most likely won't reach a large number of customers with one specific message within a short period of time. This is natural, since your message is basically sitting around waiting for people to get into a situation where it is relevant. This means that the time perspective for evaluating whether your marketing automation is delivering the financial results you're after should be considerably longer than that for a campaign (for example).

Consider *Figure 13*, which shows a simplified version of how results come in from campaigns and marketing automation. The spikes represent the value that comes from four large campaigns spread over a year. The work to produce these is put in shortly before the campaign and the results come in around the same time that each campaign runs. For the automations, however, first of all there's never really any crazy rush to get things up and running. No one will miss the modest amount of money coming from the first week of the first automated flow being run. However, the flow will continue to run, even on days when no one is at work. And if the data keeps coming in, the messages keep going out, so theoretically the investment of work keeps making you money for years. Of course, in practice you'd want to refresh the wording and the graphics, and continue to optimize the built-in logic (i.e. exactly when and why the messages are triggered). But the flow would continue to run regardless.

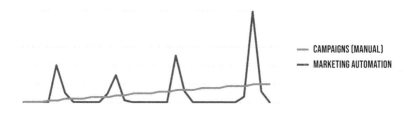

Figure 13. Value from marketing automation builds up incrementally as more automated flows are launched; value from campaigns is concentrated around blockbuster occasions.

Marketing automation gets really interesting, however, when you start to have a more elaborate battery of automated flows that each addresses customers in different important moments of truth. Then the value begins to stack up. Consider *Figure 13* again and observe the level to which value creation has risen after this fictive company has worked with marketing automation for around a year and has launched several value-creating flows that are running simultaneously. By this point, they would miss a substantial amount of money if suddenly they stopped running the flows for one reason or another. It is therefore important to remember that the value creation that comes from marketing automation is incremental and long term.

THE THREE PRIMARY VALUE DRIVERS OF MARKETING AUTOMATION

Value creation in marketing automation can be divided into three major categories:

1. Increased top line (margin)
2. Decreased customer churn
3. Cost savings

The way in which increased top-line sales are affected by marketing automation varies greatly between transactionally oriented businesses (e.g. retail and travel) and subscription businesses (e.g. streaming and entertainment, and charities to some extent). As such, the first category can be divided into two subtypes: retail and subscription.

INCREASED TOP LINE – RETAIL

For retail businesses that have few ongoing interactions with their customers, it is very important to create interactions that can supply a stream of data to determine moment-of-truth insights and thus fuel marketing automation. A grocery store (a high-purchase-frequency business) needs to do little more than have some kind of loyalty scheme to get a steady stream of data, whereas an apparel or kitchenware business might benefit from using stronger campaign pressure and/or gamification tactics. If there are no conversations to listen in on, don't hesitate to start them! And while you're at it – make them fun.

Once you have an abandoned basket, products added to a wishlist, or a transaction (or preferably multiple transactions), then a lot of the potential triggers will revolve around those data points. Give advice, information, or tips about the purchased product. Ask for a review. Ask customers whether they'd like to be notified about an out-of-stock item. Again, *Make It All About Me* by Rasmus Houlind and Colin Shearer provides plenty of concrete ideas.[1]

In general, value creation will come from addressing as many moments of truth as possible, as opposed to developing multiple variants of a triggered communication. On the other hand, automated flows are generally triggered by such great signs of customer intent that it is worth having multiple steps within each flow. In your abandoned basket flow, for instance, consider having one classic abandoned basket email, then a reminder (potentially with an SMS message on top), then a follow-up email with more broad category-related messaging and recommendations, and then perhaps a bump-up in paid media bids for a little while.

When you are setting up triggers that mimic retargeting to some extent (e.g. for an abandoned basket or an abandoned browsing session), remember that you have the option to add creativity and not just provide an echo of the customer's action. So, instead of sending emails with more pushchairs to people who are already confused from having looked at too many pushchairs, consider sending an article with guidance on how to select the right pushchair. This article could provide suggestions about what to consider and when it makes sense to choose which option.

At the conference Dialogkonferansen in Gothenburg, Sweden, in 2022, representatives of the multi-brand apparel retailer Varner-Gruppen talked about the company's use of automation. They stated that, in general, marketing automation flows increased conversions by a factor of three compared to scheduled weekly newsletters.[2] In another example, the European fashion marketplace Miinto increased its gross merchandise value (a measure comparable to total sales) per customer by 31% through marketing automation.[3]

INCREASED TOP LINE – SUBSCRIPTION

An increase in the top line for subscription businesses normally means signing customers up for a more expensive subscription. Consider the PureGym example once again. The gym will be able to identify which members consistently buy a fitness product from the vending machines and pay with their membership card (so that the data is captured). The team could then easily see who might benefit from an ALL-IN subscription with one protein bar per workout included in their fixed fee. This would be a little cheaper for the member and PureGym would get a fixed income it could count on.

Like many other streaming services, the Nordic audiobook company Storytel has a family subscription. According to their Head of CRM Sales & Operations, Per Dyring Dahlberg, in the data Storytel gathers from normal subscriptions, the company can tell who has the app installed on multiple devices and also whether each account tends to consume similar or very different genres. The consumption of different genres could be an indication that two people are sharing the subscription. These people might get their recommendations mixed up and won't get the full experience, so why not make absolutely sure that these people are aware that a family subscription exists? It would likely be wise to prioritize both owned and paid media for such an audience.

A better top line on subscriptions could potentially also mean adding retail transactions on top of the subscription. The Nordic bio meal box provider Aarstiderne, for instance, has combined its weekly grocery box service with an on-top ecommerce business. Customers don't need flour or oil every week – but when they do, why not buy it from Aarstiderne and have it delivered in the same box, given that their shipping is already paid for?[4]

DECREASED CUSTOMER CHURN

Churn rates specifically relate to subscription-based services. Decreasing churn among existing subscribers is mainly a matter of making sure that they feel they are getting value for money and wish to continue their subscription. In other words, it's about getting to a point where they are using your service sufficiently. So, you should make sure you capture any data (through either digital behaviour or surveys) on how your customers are using your services and use that to motivate them to use those services frequently. If your TV streaming subscription gives customers the opportunity to stream both live and on demand, make sure customers know this and ideally ensure that they have at least tried both before their trial subscription ends. If your audiobook service gives people the opportunity to listen to unlimited books, then aim to make sure they listen to books at least twice a week by reminding them to listen and recommending interesting books for them.

We often get questions on what the best anti-churn tactics are. Ironically enough, the best anti-churn programme is very often a good onboarding programme – specifically, one that makes sure customers are using all relevant services included in their subscription. Most subscriptions have a few critical moments of truth, where cancellations or churn are higher than normal, after which the level drops to some kind of plateau. In these moments it's more important than ever that subscribers are using their subscription to a satisfactory level.

For Nordic magazine publisher Storyhouse Egmont, the critical period is not surprisingly when the trial subscription runs out and people convert to paying full price. This is a time when subscribers ask themselves whether to continue or not. If they choose to continue, then normally they stay on for a long period of time. At the conference Digital Copenhagen in 2019, Dorte Karlsson from Storyhouse Egmont showed how the company had achieved an amazing 22% decrease in churn rate thanks to a new elaborate and highly personalized welcome programme.[5]

If for some reason your customers are not using the full plan, then most likely you will have a better plan with less consumption included that they could switch to instead. In fact, a recurring 'plan check' can be a very smart tactic to get people to stay on board. Such a check can make people feel safe and assured that they are on, for instance, the right phone subscription in terms of call minutes, data allowance, and number of text messages. In a roundtable event discussing the topic of this book, Lisa Björnskär, Head of Customer Growth & Loyalty at the telecom company '3 Sverige', shared how they did just that to decrease churn, with substantial effect.[6] This kind of check doesn't have to take the form of a triggered outbound communication, however. It can also be delivered as a last-minute downgrade offer on the cancellation page. Subscribers desiring to cancel their subscription will experience how FT.com does exactly this.[7]

COST SAVINGS

Generally speaking, marketing automation is not a cost-cutting exercise. There are cases, however, where it can greatly reduce costs. In the examples below, we'll present three such cases.

We have touched upon the first to some extent already in earlier chapters – namely, using first-party data in paid media. The lowest-hanging fruit can be found by excluding existing subscribers and recent full-price buyers from paid advertising. In retail, this should be done for a while; for subscription services, it should be done for as long as a customer has a subscription. You might also bid less on paid media for a segment of bargain hunters where you generally make less money.

Another way of using first-party data to potentially save costs is to improve your targeting of customers on paid media that you believe to be in a certain moment of truth. The football club F.C. Copenhagen saw a return on advertising spend (ROAS) more than two times its normal ROAS on certain campaigns when advertising to such customers. An example of one such moment of truth is 'customers who recently bought normal game tickets multiple times'. It turns out that these customers will fairly easily understand the benefits of signing up for a ticket subscription. Obviously, the increase in effectiveness can be used to either save money or drive more conversions with the same money.[8]

For the second example, imagine that your customers tend to raise certain questions of your support department during a specific stage in their customer lifecycle. If you were to set up automated proactive outbound communication giving people the answers to these questions, you could greatly reduce the number of service calls you received. For the Norwegian broadband service provider Eidsiva Bredbånd, introducing this strategy led to a substantial decrease in service calls.[9]

It is a matter of definition whether the third example counts as a way of saving money – but, in general, automating your win-back campaigns leads to substantially lower costs per order or per acquisition (CPO). We've seen cases with CPO as low as 30% of the average. This was the case for paid social advertising with Storyhouse Egmont when it exposed its previous subscribers to win-back offers.[10] Usually, it makes sense to highlight that you realize it's been a while since you've been in touch with the customer and that your service has improved compared to what it was back then. Remember, however, that this is not the time to encourage people to try something completely different, so don't try and lure them back with a cross-sell offer. Rather, mention something that is related to their specific use of your service.

Whether you then use the reduced cost of this third example to save money or fuel extra growth, we'll leave up to you. It doesn't change the fact that it's a brilliant tactic.

BEYOND SALES – CHASING THE NEXT BEST EXPERIENCE

Within retail especially, marketing automation has been very focused on driving repeat transactions by supplying the next best offer. Algorithms have been trained to automatically match existing offers to customers based on all available customer data. So, in a newsletter, for example, the next best offer will be featured at the top for each customer, and sales associates will be incentivized to ask each customer about this offer in particular. Also, as soon as a new offer is negotiated with a supplier and created in the database, the algorithm will do its magic and score the offer against all customers. The offer will then be sent out to all customers where the match is above a certain threshold, as defined by the merchant. The decision regarding the threshold will ultimately determine the balance between scale and relevance. The higher the threshold, the less scale but the more relevance, and vice versa.

But what if the world doesn't always revolve around you selling stuff to people? What if your customer is nowhere near making any kind of purchase decision – whether due to a previous bad experience, being broke, or some other reason that you'll never know? Then the offer would change from being the 'next best offer' to 'the least irrelevant but still quite irrelevant offer'.

As we discussed in the chapter about messages (*Chapter 8*), these don't always take the form of an offer. Sometimes it's not time to sell because other actions will create more value over the long term. For example, it could be the time to ask the customer to *do something*, such as install your app, sign up for a webinar, or complete their profile. This would be equal to what is called the 'next best action' (or NBA – not to be confused with basketball associations). Sometimes an action that is relevant for the brand isn't even appropriate or isn't what generates the most value from the customer's perspective. The message might have to do with making the customer feel something or just know something that could be helpful for them in fulfilling their goals. The concept of enabling the customer to co-create value with the brand is what Forrester calls the next best experience (NBX).[11]

In *Chapter 10* we actually already covered an example of an NBX suggestion where a brand chose expected long-term value over short-term gains. In 2016, Netflix chose to send trial customers a reminder for the first upcoming payment, doubling down on the belief that this would create a good experience with the most important customers and that customers who were scared off by this weren't profitable to try and keep anyway.

NBA and NBX are especially useful in call centres and clienteling apps that sales associates use in-store. Once the service agent or sales associate has solved a customer's question or inquiry, then they will ideally have the NBX visible for this customer in particular and have the perfect guidance for how to finish off the conversation in a way that maximizes the value creation for the business. For example, 'Did you know that the wine you just bought is made from 100% organic grapes that only grow on the north side of Etna on Sicily?' or 'As you're one of our most loved customers, we've invited you to our spring collection release party – however, I don't see your RSVP?' or 'I can see our email bounced the last time we sent you a newsletter – did you change your email address lately?'

Such personal meetings between customers and service or sales associates serve as the one exception to the rule that the message is what matters the most in outbound communication. The right message, as determined by NBX algorithms, can make a big difference if you have frequent interactions with recognized customers either in support or in-store.

WHAT ARE THE MOST EFFECTIVE FLOWS?

Not everybody has data and customer insights so well sorted that they find it easy or even possible to implement NBX. That raises the question of which marketing automation flows are the most effective and thus which should be built first. The answer, of course, is that it depends. But it is always a good idea to have some sort of flow addressing an abandoned basket, order form, or sign-up flow. This will address bottom-funnel drop-offs and immediately boost conversions. The exception is if you have very few marketing consents – then you're probably better off chasing more of them. Another important flow is your welcome flow: as discussed earlier in this chapter, a thorough welcome flow can serve as a powerful introduction to your company.

If you're thorough and want to start a marketing automation project off on the right foot, then you should begin by doing a proper customer journey mapping process. This should ideally be built on sound data visualization (as briefly mentioned in *Chapter 7*) and quantitative analyses that can help you to discover where the biggest disappointments and disconnects are in the customer journey. Then fix those first!

After that it's a matter of which direction you choose – is your strategy all about short-term chasing of money? Or is it more on-brand to build long-term relationships with customers where you aren't always selling? In most cases you should consider evening out any two sales-oriented triggers with one that is more altruistic and genuinely helpful. The Red Cross in Sweden, for instance, has an automated flow with the sole purpose of saying thank you for a donation and explaining a bit about how the donation will be put to use. The 'thank you flow' played an important part in the organization increasing the number of its regular donors by 24%.[12]

MATURITY LEVELS FOR MARKETING AUTOMATION

Just like when you are personalizing your campaigns, working with personalization in marketing automation is an area you can continue to become better at. In the table below we have conceptualized three archetypical maturity levels for how you do this. You can use this table to get an idea of your approximate maturity level as well as a suggested scope for further development.

PYRAMID OF PERSONALIZATION - FRONT END

SCOPE MATURITY

MARKETING AUTOMATION

LEADER

ALGORITHMIC INCLUSION OF CONTENT FEEDS IN EMAILS
PAID MEDIA IS PART OF KEY MARKETING AUTOMATION FLOWS
CENTRAL MESSAGES AND AI-BASED CALCULATION OF NBX
BALANCE BETWEEN COMMERCIAL AND HELPFUL MESSAGES
VARIANTS OF MESSAGES PER SEGMENT
MOST CAMPAIGNS ARE AUTOMATED

INTERMEDIATE

SIMPLE RULE-BASED SUPPRESSION LOGIC
SIMPLE RULE-BASED INCLUSION OF CONTENT FEEDS IN EMAILS
MORE COMMERCIAL THAN DELIGHTFUL MOMENTS OF TRUTH IN PLAY
RULE-BASED DETERMINATION OF MOMENTS OF TRUTH ON MULTIPLE DATA TYPES
TRIGGERS BECOME LONGER FLOWS
2-3 MOST IMPORTANT MOMENTS OF TRUTH IMPLEMENTED
USING THE FULL 'BOWTIE KNOT' (SEE CHAPTER 6)

BEGINNER

MANUAL INSERTION OF PRODUCTS AS GRAPHIC SPLASH IMAGES IN EMAILS
NO MESSAGE VARIANTS FOR DIFFERENT CUSTOMER SEGMENTS
SEPARATE CONTENT, EMAILS, AND FLOWS FOR EACH COUNTRY, LANGUAGE, AND SEGMENT
PRIMARILY WEBSITE AND EMAIL DATA ARE USED IN TRIGGERS
NO TRANSACTIONAL DATA IN USE
FEW 'SINGLE EMAIL' TRIGGERS (E.G. SIGN-UP CONFIRMATION, ABANDONED BASKET)

CHAPTER 12
CONTENT, PART 2: CONTENT FEEDS

Pier Luigi's engagement team had just completed a total redesign of their strategy to get HBO Max users to consume content more often on the platform. Based on their findings, they'd noted how users' behaviour on the platform differed substantially between weekdays and weekends. They had found that users were more likely to watch whole movies during weekends, while during weekdays users were more likely to watch and complete series episodes.

It seemed like an easy win to implement simple personalization and push the right type of title on the right days. On weekdays they would showcase mainly series on users' homepages, and at weekends the homepages would be flooded with movies. This had already been implemented on the web application and was so far viewed as a successful strategy.

Had Pier been less experienced, he might have stopped there. But further research had shown that specific users actually did the opposite and watched movies on weekdays and binge-watched entire series at weekends. The right solution was to bring this down to an individual level so as to showcase the right titles for each user.

The hypothesis was that a truly personalized experience would bring additional viewership and 'stickiness' (i.e. hours per week) to the platform. Both the app and the homepage would become the equivalent of a personalized foyer for each registered user.

Pier's team started with a sandbox test, where only a pool of users would be exposed to the new experience and their usage would be compared to that of the existing static variant. Users exposed to the test would have a personalized homepage showcasing different titles based on what they and users with similar behaviour watched at specific times of the day and on specific days of the week.

After a month of experimentation, the sandbox users had a higher completion rate and, most importantly, a higher variety of titles consumed along with higher average hours per week spent on the platform – all key success factors for user retention. Expanding from the sandbox test to full implementation for all users would still take months of back-end product work, but the road to full personalization was never meant to be an easy one.

As we covered in *Chapter 6*, content that is used in personalization comes in two kinds. We've already covered the messages, where you address segments and moments of truth creatively (see *Chapters 8* and *10*). But not all content has to be created or even modified by marketers. This content is fed from other sources, such as your product information management (PIM) system, your website, your article database, your enterprise resource planning (ERP) system, and other similar sources. In the case of most retailers, the products are fed from the PIM system and the articles from the website. In the case of HBO Max, all the shows come from the underlying application database. Just like HBO Max has movies, series, and episodes, most organizations have some kind of offering at scale, such as products, courses, articles, fitness exercises, podcasts, songs, playlists, hotels, holiday homes, houses, shows, classes, events, and so on.

So, if the marketer can't modify the content, what is there to do, you may ask yourself? Well, quite a lot actually. According to the Bowtie of Personalization, the content you choose to show to specific customers should ideally match both the segments and the moments of truth of those customers. Thus, in the case of HBO Max, if it appeared that an individual user had a preference for watching movies on weekdays judging by their viewing history, then a relevant content feed of movies would be shown on weekdays.

In a brilliant YouTube video about personalizing the listening experience, Mounia Lalmas from Spotify actually refers to these separate content feeds as 'shelves' – the company has shelves of songs, albums, artists, and playlists.[1] Relating this back to the HBO Max example, Pier's team could also show a feed of similar movies to provide alternatives, with a dynamically inserted message explaining why the movies were being shown, such as 'Because you watched $TitleName'. This would provide the customer with some context to enable them to better understand why each feed was being shown.

The customer's first clicks or interactions on a web page (a product search, for instance) will quickly reveal more about their intent. In *Chapter 11* we discussed how the message is the most important part to personalize when you are working outbound – in other words, sending messages out to customers through either owned media or paid advertising (search marketing excluded, since a search with intent is needed to initiate these ads). This doesn't mean that emails should not include content feeds, but obviously they fit poorly into a subject line or a text message, to say the least. That's why personalizing content feeds is more of a big deal when working inbound.

USING CONTENT PROPERTIES TO GROUP, SORT, RANK, FILTER, AND MARK

Within each type of content feed, the content bits will share the same format and properties. For instance, products might all have a name, a category, a brand name, a colour, a size, product images, and so on. Articles could all have a title, an excerpt, a header image, a URL, body text, and so on. You can provide great value as a marketer by deciding how to group, sort, rank, filter, and mark content when presenting it to customers of different segments and in different moments of truth.

GENERIC GROUPING OF CONTENT

Grouping products is about selecting and showing products that share the same properties to make navigation easy. The most common version would be to show a specific category of products (e.g. underwear or men's clothes). Sometimes the category correlates strongly with your top segments. Someone browsing for children's clothing has a strong likelihood of belonging to your 'parents segment'.

More detailed content groups can relate to colour, type, style, occasion, and need. If you've done your user-centred research for the website properly then the specific options available for style, occasion, and need should match the most important moments of truth in your customer journey.

Your high-level content groups will most likely map one-to-one onto most or even all of the category pages on your website or the screens in your app. You might then allow customers to browse your full product catalogue based on gender (e.g. on HM.com), occasion (e.g. weddings, anniversaries, or funerals when browsing flower gifts on Interflora.com), or 'concern' (e.g. dryness, acne, or fine lines when browsing beauty products on Sephora.com).

Behavioural data indicating extensive clicking and browsing of these category pages can provide powerful indications of customer intent and trigger communications that serve relevant content and advice. So if, for instance, you've seen customers browsing the 'dry skin' section of your website, you can follow up with a personalized message about how to relieve dry skin and a feed of articles and products that can help these customers do so. Another idea would be to group products for which there is an attractive discount at a given time and periodically send these super-discounts out to a segment of customers who have consistently bought stuff on sale.

ADVANCED GROUPING OF CONTENT

Another dynamic way of grouping the content in a feed is by personal relation to the content. In the HBO app, this would be the groups carrying headlines such as 'My List', 'Continue Watching', or even 'For You'. The first two clearly aren't algorithmically determined but a reminder of something the customer already did. They function in the same way as a wishlist, a list of favourites, a list of products in an abandoned basket, or a list of previously bought products. They are highly personalized but are intended to encourage frequency as opposed to inspiration.

The content shown in HBO Max's 'For You' is clearly the result of an algorithm, though. Based on previous data, this is the algorithm's best guess about which shows you will next want to watch across all categories. If the algorithm has very little data to work with for one specific customer, the suggested shows will most likely resemble the list of generally popular shows.

Perhaps you've also noticed 'Because you watched $TitleName' as a headline for a group of shows in your preferred streaming app. In this case there is something deeper at play. Based on a similarity matrix for all shows (i.e. data on which shows are most often watched by the same people), the algorithm picks one of the shows or series you watched the most and recommends series that are closely related to this show in particular. Imagine the total number of potential combinations at play here – all shows related to all other shows.

The retail version of 'Because you watched $TitleName' is the product feeds that appear on product detail pages and shopping basket pages. Typically, they appear below the actual product or basket in question. In the first content feed shown on a product details page, you'll normally want to show alternatives to the product and, immediately below that, complementary products such as accessories. On the basket page, you'll remove any friction and not raise any unnecessary doubt. So, assuming the products are the right ones for the customer, you'll try to optimize basket size by leaving out substitutional products and showing complementary ones. The headline could almost be 'Products in baskets similar to yours'.

Speaking of headlines, the importance of an insightful headline should not be neglected. An experiment conducted by Martin Jonassen, former Head of Intelligence at the Swedish audiobook company Storytel, saw a 30% uplift in performance (measured in clicks) from a feed of audiobooks when the headline was changed to 'Because you $RecommendationReason' as opposed to just 'Popular'.[2] This is clearly a case where explicit personalization beats implicit personalization.

SORTING AND RANKING

Naturally, properties can also be used to sort products and other content within a feed. On most ecommerce sites the default sorting will be the opaque option of 'sort by relevance'. If there is a product recommendation tool at play, then this will algorithmically determine the sorting on an individual basis. Provided that there is any unique data to use, this will be different from customer to customer. Clicking around a few category pages, searching a bit, and adding a few products to a wishlist should ultimately change the ranking of products within a product feed on a category page (for example). If there are few data points available – or if there is no algorithm to do the sorting – then there will be a strong resemblance between sorting by relevance and sorting by popularity.

For a website, all you need to do is decide on the default sorting and the customer can then later change (customize) it. In an email, obviously you have to decide on the one parameter on which to sort the content. Relevance is a good default – but perhaps include a second block aimed at the segment of bargain hunters with a content feed that is sorted by discount showing them the best current deals.

FILTERING

Customers mostly use filtering to customize the content shown on a category page of a website or app, or on a search results page. Customers can filter based on available sizes, brands, subcategories, and so on. This is essentially customization and not personalization. Each time a filter is set, however, this creates a new virtual subcategory page that says something about the customer's intent, which can then be used to re-engage the customer if nothing ends up in their basket.

An outbound message following up on such a browsing session would typically include a more or less similar filtering of the products. If you have the content for it, then the message could also include more information on the category or brand. You might also include a buying guide, which could actually help the customer move closer to a purchasing decision and not just show an echo of what they were already looking at. If a customer has looked at 50 or more kitchen mixers, it won't be extra product options that will drive them closer to a purchase. A buying guide might, however!

When working with content feeds in outbound communication (such as emails), you might want to consider additional filtering. Beware, here, of the danger of being considered creepy or inappropriate (see *Chapter 4*). Consider which products you do not wish to send out because they could either hurt someone's feelings or be considered inappropriate. For instance, Matas.dk sells health and beauty products, including intimate vibrators. These products would never be included in a triggered product recommendation as they have been filtered out.[3] Who wants to risk receiving an email with an extensive list of vibrators while they are at work? Very few people. They could, however, be snuck in as one interesting product in a more diverse mix of products. This method is closely related to the example of the American retailer Target, discussed in *Chapter 3*. If your products or your message could be perceived as controversial, hurtful, or just plain embarrassing, then be more subtle and implicit in the way you present the content.

MARKING

One last way of using properties is to highlight content that shares certain properties. For example, this can be done by dynamically putting an 'eco' label on all products in a feed that are produced ecologically or marking all products that are on sale with a discount ribbon. Or, as in the case of the Danish ecommerce grocery store Nemlig.com, you could personalize the product feed by highlighting previously bought products for the individual customer with a small heart.

In *Chapter 9*, we discussed retail media as a way of creating an extra revenue stream for many companies. In most countries it is required by law to mark sponsored product listings with a small 'sponsored' label in line with the product listing.

PERSONALIZING CONTENT FEEDS

Many of the above tactics don't necessary involve personalization. Customers who visit inbound platforms (such as websites and apps) already have an intention when they do so. And a large part of your work as a marketer is to reduce friction for customers trying to do what they intend to do.

In general, customers will be okay with navigating a website to the category they wish to browse. As Amazon has clearly proven, though, including personalized product recommendations on a website can greatly improve performance. McKinsey has estimated that as early as 2013, 35% of Amazon's sales came from personalized recommendations.[4] Needless to say, Amazon has continued working on its proprietary algorithm since then.

It is not the purpose of this book to deep dive into the inner workings of the algorithms in use as this is a whole science in itself. If you think about it, however, there are many personalization tactics to consider when you include content feeds as an element within personalization. We've even come across a company that supported its sustainability agenda by training algorithms to mix vegetable burgers into the product category for minced meat and barbecue products.

If you can determine where in the customer lifecycle a specific customer is – namely, which moment of truth they are in – then you can group or filter the content feeds you show accordingly. So, imagine you have a shopper on your website of your sport show brand, and your insights indicate that she is in an explorative mindset, perhaps browsing the men's section loosely. Your algorithm should carefully check out which categories she is most likely to buy from and, in a follow-up email, include products from those categories. If you've also figured out that based on her full purchase history, she is part of the gift shopper segment, then why not include a group of products that are commonly bought as gifts within a comparable price range to further help her on her way?

Carefully consider how to present your content feeds based on both segments and moments of truth. And carefully consider *which* content feeds to show, hide, or prioritize over others.

THE RIGHT FEED MEANS MORE THAN THE RANKING WITHIN IT

Imagine you're in a store. What is more frustrating – not being able to find the right shelf or not being able to find the right product on that shelf? As consumers we're okay with browsing a little if we believe we are looking on the right shelf – it could even be that finding a specific brand of pesto didn't mean that much to us after all. That's why it's more important to show and label the optimal content feeds than it is to rank the content bits within the feeds. Pier Luigi's team – at the beginning of this chapter – discovered this when they did some additional research. Conventional wisdom would suggest that consistency would be important for users, but it turned out that this wasn't the case. Through testing, HBO Max found that it achieved better performance by personalizing not only the ranking of shows within specific rows but also the sorting of the rows themselves.

Taking the lessons from this example into outbound communication (e.g. email) makes the point kind of obvious. In an email, you have static content feeds (made static at the moment they are sent out), so you need to think carefully about which content feeds to include depending on both the segment and the moment of truth. Don't send a customer a Black Friday email with a feed of women's offers if you know they normally shop men's. Don't send an offer relating to mountain bikes if a customer has only ever shown interest in road bikes. These are essentially the same as 'floating rows'. You have to make a personalization decision about which rows to include in each particular occasion and context.

ECHO CHAMBERS OR SOURCES OF INSPIRATION?

In the public debate around social media, the terms 'filter bubbles' and 'echo chambers' have seen the light of day. They refer to the fact that we as human beings feel better and less challenged if we aren't presented with information or content that is too far from our preferences and thus creates cognitive dissonance. The criticism is that on Facebook, for instance, the algorithm will slowly filter out posts that don't resonate with our political beliefs.[5] The algorithm supposedly does this simply by watching how we like and comment over time (i.e. gauging our positive and negative sentiment) and slowly showing us more and more posts from people we already agree with. Ultimately, we are no longer presented with opinions that differ much from our own.

If we take this analogy into how we work with personalization of content feeds, there are some similarities. For example, Spotify has proven that the same mechanisms around cognitive dissonance also apply to which songs we prefer in recommendations.[6] The more artists diverge from what users normally listen to, the lower the satisfaction when these are recommended. But there's a sweet spot where a certain amount of diversity is okay and doesn't compromise satisfaction too much.

This knowledge can be used in personalization tactics – for instance, in retail when sending out 'we miss you' emails. It teaches us that for those customers where we are lacking frequency, we should select products and offers that are closely related to their previous history (from within their filter bubble) so as to create as little cognitive dissonance as possible in encouraging them to come back. For the customers where we don't have an issue with frequency but where we are lacking share-of-wallet (i.e. where customers are spending more on other brands), we can instead try our luck with recommending products from other categories.

There needs to be a careful balance, though – you need to experiment and find the right level of diversity. Of all your products that a customer is *less likely* to be interested in, which are they *most likely* to buy (and thus, which are most likely to improve their customer lifetime value)? If you're able to convince high-frequency buyers to start buying from another category of your inventory, you can potentially increase their customer lifetime value to a whole new level.

In order to optimize value in both the short term and the long term – in all emails and on all high-level category pages – you should consider including multiple content feeds that are more or less diverse or relevant in what they contain.

USING CONTENT FEEDS WISELY

Content feeds are very important for delivering value to customers on all inbound platforms. Not all feeds need to be personalized, however, as there will always be people interested in 'new products' or 'top sellers'. The most important thing to personalize is *which* feeds to include in your communications and making that selection personalized – not showing the same feeds to everyone. Personalized content feeds are also important when working with outbound communication. However, they are not as important as the message that encourages the recipient to open an email or tap on a notification.

CHAPTER 13
PERSONALIZATION ON INBOUND PLATFORMS

Visitors to your website have an intention to come there. If you've done your homework with smart campaigns (*Chapter 9*) and marketing automation (*Chapter 11*), then it may even have been you who sparked or nurtured that intention. This chapter explores the third and final major marketing discipline: personalization on inbound platforms. As we covered in the previous chapter, this does include personalization of content feeds, but that is far from all there is to it.

RELATING INBOUND PLATFORM CONSTRUCTION TO THE BOWTIE OF PERSONALIZATION

The way you construct your inbound platforms is strongly related to the Bowtie of Personalization. Good websites and apps are constructed based on customer insights. Some of these insights should come from qualitative studies and form the background of your ability to interpret the more quantitative insights. Quantitative insights can take the form of either segments or more dynamic moments of truth. Website navigation and structure normally reflect both types of insight, and across your various web pages you will show both messages and content feeds.

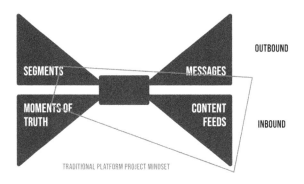

Figure 14. The structure of inbound platforms relates closely to the Bowtie of Personalization; personalization on inbound platforms normally starts with content feeds.

However, while the structure of an inbound platform is clearly related to the Bowtie of Personalization, this doesn't mean that all content is necessarily personalized dynamically or that there have to be big differences in which content is shown to which users. In this chapter we'll dig a little deeper into how inbound platforms are created, before moving on to consider what is most commonly personalized on inbound platforms – and in what order – and what effects this can get you (i.e. the value you can create).

CREATING INBOUND PLATFORMS FROM INSIGHTS

Constructing a new website or app is often a very big project – not only in terms of developing functionality and integrations with other platforms in your marketing technology stack (martech stack) but also in terms of creating the bulk of the content and functionality. This is the case even if there is little to no personalization going on. When deciding which functionality and content to prioritize, however, both insight parts of the Bowtie of Personalization come into play. Which of your primary segments are using the platform? Should you develop personas for them to make it easier for your team to relate to customers and their needs? How about the various moments of truth? These will be reflected in the navigation and in the prioritized functionality. For instance, clicking 'Dryness' below 'Shop by concern' on Sephora.com is an example of how a user can navigate towards a certain product selection, namely skin lotion for dry skin. In turn, this provides Sephora.com with the insight that users navigating here are most likely to be in a certain moment of truth. Menu items should reflect the most common moments of truth as well as the most common customer segments.

A website will also often have multiple landing pages, as not everyone will start their browsing session on the homepage. Instead, they may be directed from a piece of outbound communication to a landing page where all content is designed specifically for a certain moment of truth or segment. Although the page itself is not necessarily personalized dynamically, it still plays an important part in a personalized customer experience.

CORE CUSTOMER EXPERIENCE COMES BEFORE PERSONALIZATION

Part III goes into detail about essential prerequisites for personalization. However, a point worth highlighting here is that the core interaction design and the user experience (UX) of inbound platforms are more important than personalizing them. As any website or app is 'self-service', getting the right features and content on the website or in the app is far more important than personalizing it to segments or individual customers. This includes giving customers the option of customizing content feeds and search results – you should do this before implementing personalization.

As a consequence, a lot of the content on a website is generally not personalized – with the exception, of course, of pages such as 'My Profile' or 'My $Brand', which are visible solely to logged-in users. Your company story, corporate information, 'About Us' section, and so on won't differ depending on which user is looking at them. And, as we argue in *Chapter 2*, you should stand firm on your identity and not personalize your brand story.

PERSONALIZATION IN NEAR REAL TIME

When the core customer experience of your platforms is in place and it is time to personalize the experience for specific customers as opposed to optimizing it for the masses, keep in mind that your inbound platforms are the most responsive and real-time channels you have (at least, if you don't count the personal interactions you have with your customers on the phone and in real life). You need to count on your staff to do what's right in these situations, but on your digital platforms this means that personalization has to happen at a much faster pace in order to make a difference. Personalization engines have to deliver their output in near real time if they are to make any difference – for anonymous users, they must respond based on the clickstream and searches in the past ten seconds (for example) of the current session.

Returning to an example introduced in *Chapter 10*, if you suddenly have a northern-hemisphere user browsing for a bikini in February with no previous signs of this intent, then you'd better act fast or she'll buy that bikini somewhere else. If you try to capture her attention with a perfectly designed message that does not support her intent, you'll most likely fail.

PERSONALIZING CONTENT FEEDS VS PERSONALIZING MESSAGES

That said, not all personalization has to be done in real time, of course. Any personalization of messages based on your rather static segments can also make a bit of a difference. However, the primary attraction of your platforms is most likely your content feeds, and customers will have come to your platforms for a reason and with an intention. Therefore, keep in mind that a front-page banner or category-page banner with a personalized offer or call to action will most likely lose the battle for your customers' attention to the personalized content feeds right below.

There is one exception to this rule of thumb, however – namely, a prompt to unlock gated content. This is essentially a personalized message to everyone who has 'reached their daily quota' of free articles or similar.

THE ORDER OF PERSONALIZATION ON INBOUND PLATFORMS

Once you've decided to invest in personalization on your website or app, you should take care to design features, functionality, and content in accordance with key segments and typical moments of truth in your customers' journey. You may not get it right on your first go, but continuous optimization of both conversion rates and softer metrics such as customer satisfaction will take you further than you might imagine.

START WITH 'MY' PAGES

The first thing to actually personalize is the 'My account' page (or whatever you decide to call your pages designed for logged-in customers). Showing customers' own data (e.g. their transactions, payments, and any other history) on these pages is personalization by default, even though it may not feel like it.

PERSONALIZE CONTENT FEEDS

Once you do start personalizing further, you'll begin by addressing content feeds. This assumes that you have content feeds that are key and relevant to your business. A consultancy will not necessarily have a lot of content feeds and nor will an insurance company – except if they have a multitude of articles that their visitors find important. Remember that on inbound platforms, getting the right content feeds in the right places matters far more than getting the ranking of each item with a content feed in place.

ADD PERSONALIZED MESSAGES

Once you're done with personalizing your content feeds (we know you don't really reach the point of being 'done', but play with the thought just for now), then comes the personalization of your messages based on segments and moments of truth.

Personalizing your messages based on moments of truth will create higher engagement and is really where you should ultimately be heading. Ultimately, you should be using every window of opportunity and every place where you have your customers' attention to tell them about the next best experience (NBX) (see *Chapter 11*).

To begin with, however, personalizing your messages by segment will most likely make things easier for you in terms of managing internal stakeholders. This is because internal stakeholders often fight over who gets to 'have the front page'. It can therefore be a great relief to enable personalization and allow multiple stakeholders to 'own' the key message on the front page or on category pages simultaneously by supplying segment criteria along with their own content.

HIDING UNNECESSARY CONTENT IS ALSO PERSONALIZATION

An opportunity that is overlooked far too often is to hide irrelevant messages and elements that create unnecessary friction for customers. If, for instance, you have a known customer on your website who the algorithm suggests isn't ready to make a purchase but is merely gathering inspiration, then consider hiding all the classic nudges around scarcity and time-limited offers as they would be wasted. If the algorithm is right, you'd just be creating friction by showing these. In principle, this is incorporated into the ideas behind the NBX, but the 'messages' here are quite often thought of as functionality and thus not subject to personalization.

You can also choose to hide certain second-level menu items if insights show that these are irrelevant for a specific customer.

VALUE CREATION FROM PERSONALIZATION ON INBOUND PLATFORMS

The good thing about implementing personalization on a well-designed and already conversion-optimized website with a high traffic volume is that the initial effect is near instant. If, on the other hand, you don't have sufficient traffic, then get that right before doing any optimization, let alone personalization. Advertising, traditional public relations work, and search engine optimization will help you get there.

INCREASING TOP-LINE SALES

Needless to say, presenting more relevant products to your customers will make more of them add products to their basket and purchase them – whether it be from the front page, a category page, a product detail page, search results, or the basket itself. The same goes for the streaming shows or the news articles that customers consume during a trial period. The better the customer's experience of the content feeds, the higher the engagement and the higher the rate of conversion to a paid membership.

Clever messaging can, of course, also make a difference in terms of when and how to ask for a paid subscription while clearly communicating the benefits, the different plans, and the options. For large bodies of content, working with personalization can also mean that a much larger share of news articles (for instance) makes it to the front pages and thus more content is activated. To handle this, the inbound platform simply gets increased capacity so it can activate more content. If you are selling advertising space, this means that you can have more inventory and thus make more money from advertisers because you can serve a larger customer base.

As a result of personalizing their product feeds, the team at Miinto have succeeded in creating an increase of 11% in revenue per visit based on a 6% uplift in conversion rates and a 5% higher average order value.[1] Given the fact that these tactics do not require manual maintenance, this is a permanent addition to an already sound revenue stream. In addition to working with personalization on their website, they also integrate specific product feeds into Google's and Facebook's shopping platforms. In this way, they have essentially moved some of their customers' initial shopping experience onto the big tech giants' platforms. Specific product feeds can be defined and matched with advertising audiences that are built using either the data of the advertising platforms or first-party data.

REDUCING SERVICE COSTS

Dynamic personalization of on-site messages can also be a huge cost-saver. An example of this comes from the Swedish grocery store chain Coop.[2] When the company sold groceries online, the products were picked by hand and fulfilled from the nearest outlet. For certain categories of products, however, the stores might not have a lot of stock. If a large number of these products were added to the basket, a simple on-site alert would ask the customer to call customer service to check the availability. In this way, frustrations were fewer and friction was reduced.

REDUCING CHURN

We mentioned in *Chapter 11* how a cross-sell to a new product category must be handled carefully: on the one hand, it is harder than getting customers to buy more of the same product, but on the other hand, it has the potential to increase customer lifetime value substantially. For streaming services, the same logic applies. If a customer streams both the 'Shows' category and the 'Football' category, then there's a lower chance of them cancelling their subscription. They may have come for the football, but they stay for other categories once the football is on its break.

MATURITY LEVELS FOR PERSONALIZATION ON INBOUND PLATFORMS

When you are working with personalization on inbound platforms such as websites and apps, personalization tends to become a priority a bit further down the road than when you are working with campaigns and marketing automation. Once you become advanced, though, there's a gradual shift towards centralized combination of insights and content, and on creating messages that are focused on customer intent as opposed to the next best offer or discount.

In the table below, we've conceptualized three maturity levels for working with personalization on inbound platforms to help you evaluate your current level and where to take it from here.

PYRAMID OF PERSONALIZATION - FRONT END

SCOPE MATURITY

INBOUND PLATFORMS

LEADER
PERSONALIZED MESSAGES INCORPORATED ACROSS ALL INBOUND PLATFORMS
USE OF CENTRAL PERSONALIZED MESSAGES AND INSIGHTS (NBX)
CONTENT FEEDS MATCHING MOMENTS OF TRUTH DYNAMICALLY CREATED USING AI
CONTENT FEEDS RANKED AND CREATED DYNAMICALLY PER INDIVIDUAL CUSTOMER USING AI

INTERMEDIATE
PERSONALIZATION FOR BOTH KNOWN AND UNKNOWN CUSTOMERS
SIMPLE RULE-BASED PERSONALIZATION OF FRONT-PAGE HERO MESSAGE
CENTRALIZED MANAGEMENT OF PRODUCT AND CONTENT FEEDS
ALGORITHMIC RANKING OF PRODUCTS PER CUSTOMER WITHIN CATEGORIES USING AI

BEGINNER
MANUAL MANAGEMENT OF ASSOCIATIONS BETWEEN PRODUCTS AND CONTENT
RANKING OF PRODUCTS AND CONTENT BASED ON GENERAL POPULARITY
PERSONALIZATION APPLIES FOR KNOWN CUSTOMERS ONLY
PERSONALIZATION ONLY HAPPENS BEHIND A LOG-IN ('MY ACCOUNT')
CONVERSION RATE OPTIMIZATION (CRO) IS THE FOCUS OF THE WEBSITE TEAM

CHAPTER 14
TYING IT ALL UP IN THE BOWTIE OF PERSONALIZATION

In previous chapters we've covered all four corners of the Bowtie of Personalization and explored how you can benefit from working with personalization in the three major marketing disciplines: through campaigns, through marketing automation, and on inbound platforms. You should now have a deep understanding of what personalization is and how the insights and the content ends of the Bowtie of Personalization can be tied together in a beautiful, personalized knot. As *Figure 15* shows, your segments are the insights that matter the most when you are working with campaigns. Moments of truth matter the most when you are working with marketing automation. The content that matters the most when you are working with outbound communication is your messages. And if you are working with personalization on inbound platforms, you should be most concerned with personalizing your content feeds.

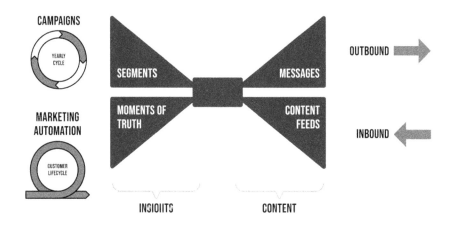

Figure 15. Each corner of the bowtie has its primary use case.

Combining all four corners of the bowtie simultaneously is (k)not easy. However, when you do so, everything is centred around your customers at a specific moment and you can expect a substantial lift in their perception of the customer experience.

In this chapter, after revisiting the knot in the bowtie, we'll explore what a realistic 'good' customer journey looks like when you become a leader within personalization. We will then spend some time diving into how you measure the value that we have been talking so much about. It turns out that *how* you measure isn't a given, but it has a tremendous impact on how you create value and how you can keep yourself and your team creating positive impact and results. At the end of the chapter, we'll gather the maturity levels for personalization within campaigns (*Chapter 9*), marketing automation (*Chapter 11*), and inbound platforms (*Chapter 13*) into the front end of the Pyramid of Personalization, which we introduced briefly in *Chapter 6*.

With the front end of the Pyramid of Personalization at hand, you'll have a tool to help you make better decisions about the scope of any personalization-related project, including what is normally done in which order. Together with the case studies from *Chapters 9, 11*, and *13*, this will help you to set realistic expectations both within your team and among senior management.

GETTING BACK TO THE KNOT OF THE BOWTIE

Back in *Chapter 6*, before we got into the details of the Bowtie of Personalization, we discussed how the central knot is an analogy for the moment that all your personalization efforts come together at the same time. When you combine insights such as segments and moments of truth with corresponding content in the form of creative messages and content feeds, you get as close as possible to hyper-personalization. Doing so creates a truly memorable and differentiating customer experience – one that will win you not only money, but customers' hearts as well.

However, the goal is not to always be hyper-personalized for all customers on all channels, as this is simply not feasible and would require you to do tremendous amounts of work in discovering insights, producing content, and matching that content to customers according to expected perception of relevance. There will always be prospects and customers about whom you know very little, and thus in those cases your chances of being hyper-personalized will be slim to none.

WHAT DOES 'GOOD' LOOK LIKE FROM THE CUSTOMER'S POINT OF VIEW?

How good can a personalized customer experience actually get? Set aside the 'golden moments' potentially captured in the knot of the bowtie – for now we're talking about the general customer experience over time.

Imagine that you've mastered all the techniques that we've covered so far in this book. What, then, what would an individual customer journey look like? On a granular level, there would really be no telling up front. As we've discussed, no matter how many data points we have for a specific customer, we still only see a fraction of the full picture. So much is going on in customers' lives about which we don't have any data, and we never really know what's on somebody's mind. So, the customer journey belongs to the customer.

CUSTOMER JOURNEY $=$ YOUR MARKETING $+$ EVERYTHING ELSE IN THE CUSTOMER'S LIFE

We as marketers can only try to nudge the journey in the direction we believe will benefit us by benefitting the customer. For each personalized touchpoint we increase our chances of making this happen, but we can never expect our communication to be perceived as 100% relevant all the time.

In a specific customer's journey, they will definitely experience a lot of the personalized content you've put together. But because you can't always sit around waiting for customers to come to you, this specific person will also experience some of your more general marketing and communication – across all channels. Your marketing contribution to an individual customer journey is thus a mix of highly personalized communication, semi-personalized communication, and generic unpersonalized communication. This will be made up of brand advertising, performance marketing, editorial newsletters, triggered app notifications, and automated emails. *Figure 16* gives an example of how a customer might encounter different types of communication along the customer journey.

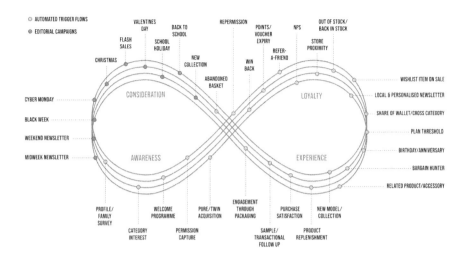

Figure 16. Typical retail customer journey from 'Awareness' to 'Consideration', 'Experience', and 'Loyalty'; along the way, a customer experiences marketing and communication from both campaigns and marketing automation.

The personalized customer experience, therefore, cannot always be hyper-personalized and 'remain in the knot of the bowtie' all the time, so to speak. And even when personalization is going well, the customer won't necessarily always notice. Their segment may have been excluded from specific communication, or some of the personalization may be implicit and thus designed to be subtle and discreet.

THE REALISTIC END GOAL OF THE PERSONALIZED CUSTOMER EXPERIENCE

So, given the knowledge that we've gained in this book so far, let's try to sum up what characterizes a realistic personalized customer journey for an engaged customer in a company that is a leader in personalization.

First of all, we have the so-called hygiene factors (things customers expect as standard). The customer can actively log in and remain logged in. When they change channels, they never have to start over and aren't asked to resubmit any information previously given in any other channel. They are in full control of any marketing and data consents and can easily revoke them. The basic user experience of the website and the app is fairly frictionless, and the standard functionality is available and intuitive.

With regard to marketing communication, the customer sees no advertisements or any other marketing communication for products they recently bought or subscriptions they already have. In general, and as long as they stay engaged with the brand, they primarily receive communication on owned media. The offers and promotions they receive are mostly seen as relevant and are consistent across the various communication channels. They are gently reminded to complete already initiated and/or necessary tasks to maximize the value of their customer relationship (either by taking advantage of offers or by using services and products they have already paid for to get maximum value). This means that a large portion of the messages are unrelated to sales.

The customer does not perceive all inspirational messages and content feeds to be 100% relevant. Some are, but others sit right around the edge of what the customer would normally engage with. When they are not ready to make a purchase, they are not pushed or nudged to do so. They only see content feeds on category pages and in emails that are relevant (or, at least, not irrelevant), and the ranking of the elements therein seems to have put the most interesting elements first.

LESS ENGAGED CUSTOMERS WILL EXPERIENCE LESS PERSONALIZATION

Even if you've built a marketing set-up to support the above ideal scenario, it doesn't mean that it will apply to all customers. The amount of historical and recent data for each customer will set the bar for how personalized a customer experience that person can expect to have. It's the same as in real life – if you know nothing about the person sitting next to you, you have to either ask or talk about yourself. Or wait around for things to happen – but this is hardly a sound business strategy.

We believe that a lot of the critique and scepticism around personalization has its roots in this very insight. You will never be hyper-personalized for everybody all the time. But that doesn't mean you shouldn't aspire to deliver a more personalized customer experience than today. There's still a lot of value to bring to customers and your company.

MEASURING THE VALUE OF PERSONALIZATION

In describing the primary marketing disciplines that involve personalization, we have already mentioned several potential uplifts. During these discussions, we've somewhat casually thrown various metrics and key performance indicators (KPIs) around. Before moving on to discuss prerequisites in *Part III* and organizational matters in *Part IV*, we'd like to zoom in on how to measure success from personalization.

Measuring success from personalization relates to the three maturity levels in the pyramid. Practitioners will tend to focus on different types of metrics based on their maturity level. Beginners will focus on channel-specific engagement metrics such as click rates and reach. Intermediates will focus on conversions and sales. Leaders will focus on customer metrics such as customer lifetime value (CLV) and net promoter score (NPS). CLV is an economic figure representing how much value a single customer will most likely provide to a company as long as the customer relationship remains intact. NPS is closely related to customer satisfaction and is thus an emotional metric. Instead of measuring satisfaction directly, NPS focuses on the customer's willingness to recommend a product or service. So, in that sense, NPS goes one level beyond satisfaction into ambassadorship.

This evolution of metrics is a reflection of the common marketing evolution from engagement to sales to customer-centricity.[1]

IDENTIFYING YOUR METRICS

You have probably tried testing and measuring the effects of different subject lines in emails. This is basically a type of conversion rate optimization (CRO). It is about trying to find the one generic subject line that outperforms the rest. You have probably also compared your conversion rates for automated emails with your conversion rates for campaign emails and counted the total sales generated by a personalized campaign. But what is the right way to measure the success of personalization efforts?

First of all, it isn't *wrong* to do any of the above. Most of the time, better engagement metrics (such as clicks and opens) do eventually have an effect on conversion rates and ultimately CLV. It is also interesting to look at the total sales for a personalized campaign compared to the equivalent from last year. But a myopic focus on click rates can juke the stats and create worthless suboptimization. Moreover, so many things change contextually from year to year – in terms of what stimulates sales and customer engagement – that it's often quite difficult to compare campaign results like for like.

More importantly, however, none of these measurement tactics answers the question of whether the personalization was worth it. You need to ask yourself what the generic alternative to the personalized version of your efforts is. Sometimes it's just a generic piece of content. Sometimes it's doing nothing at all. Once you have identified what is appropriate, you can move on to testing using a control group.

USING CONTROL GROUPS

To compare your personalization efforts with their generic alternatives, you need to define a control group. A control group is normally a small portion (e.g. 5–10%) of your customer database that you choose to expose to the generic alternative. In this book, we'll call the other group the dialogue group. In the case of launching a marketing automation flow, the control group might not be exposed to the flow at all. That way, you can test the effect of the whole flow, including all personalized aspects.

After an appropriate time period has passed, you can compare the results for the two groups. If you've done well, you should see a difference in the share of customers who performed the action you wanted them to do – hopefully in favour of the dialogue group.

However, in order not to draw any false conclusions, you need what is called 'statistical significance' before you can conclude which group is the winner. To put it simply, this means that enough people must have been exposed to your personalization experiment to ensure that the numbers are steady and wouldn't change much if more people were included. For a short campaign, the size of the control group will determine whether you'll get statistical significance or not. For a marketing automation flow, both the size of the control group and the amount of time it has been running will be the determinants. It's essential to get statistical significance

– and it's good to get it quickly. In that way, you can try out more things and learn more quickly.

Calculating the appropriate size of a control group can be difficult, though, so we recommend you use one of the many online tools for doing this. In the following example, we've used Optimizely's Sample Size Calculator.[2] As an example, let's say you have a simple automated email welcome flow for trial subscribers with the aim of converting them to your full paid subscription. If the original conversion rate is 30% and you're aiming to lift this by at least 20% (to a new conversion rate of 36%), then you need to let the flow run until you've had 580 control group members through the new flow, plus at least the same number of test group members. So if you have 1,160 new trial members daily, the experiment would be over as soon as these people had been through your welcome flow. If the uplift turns out to be smaller than the 20%, you'd need to let the experiment run longer before you can draw a conclusion with 95% certainty, which is normally an accepted rate for calculating control group (sample) sizes.

Using control groups comes with a caveat, though: the people in the control group won't get the better, more personalized experience. In that sense, it actually costs you money to deploy a control group. For this reason, control groups shouldn't necessarily be permanent and static. For example, let's say you've done your control group work on your welcome email flow and you've proven there is a 20% difference in terms of sales between the control group and the dialogue group. You could then either make the control group smaller and keep it like that to have fresh numbers, or consider not having it any more. Keep the report on the results of your experiment in a drawer, though. Most likely, someday a finance manager will come and try to kill your personalized flows and take your headcount and software to help cut costs. And even if no one asks, you're still better off knowing how much you're saving or earning by using personalization.

USING PROXY METRICS

As you become more advanced with your personalization (i.e. as you move up the maturity levels) metrics become more customer-centric. However, it can be tricky to take these measurements. For example, in the case of CLV, when is the customer relationship over? When can you expect a customer to 'not spend' any more? When has a retail customer 'churned'?

We shall once again turn to the work of Gibson Biddle, former Vice President of Product at Netflix. He suggests that when it would take a long time to get the real metrics and make decisions on the back of them, you should use so-called proxy metrics.[3] When Netflix wanted to measure the effect of a new content recommendation algorithm, it could have used churn statistics. However, instead, the company measured how many customers with the old algorithm spent 40 or more hours per month watching shows on Netflix, versus the number of customers with the new algorithm. The number 40 wasn't picked randomly, of course – it was determined through a churn analysis showing that customers using the service above this limit had a substantially lower chance of terminating their subscription. This served as a good proxy metric for churn risk, but it was easier and quicker to collect and calculate.

DO THE MATH – ALL THE WAY TO THE MONEY

Once you've achieved your statistically significant results on whether the personalized or the generic experience is most effective, you'll face a further challenge: presenting your results in a way that will earn you trust and potentially extra resources from senior management. For this to play out the way you want it to, we suggest that you don't present engagement metrics, or even conversion rates, as these can be hard for senior managers to relate to. Instead, we suggest that you do the math and calculate how many people the improved conversion rate applied to, how much they spent, and what the margin was on the goods they bought. In other words – do the math until you can count the money the difference makes. And money is a language that all senior executives understand.

Doing this math on expected potential outcome before an experiment or a project is implemented can even help you determine how much you can invest without the risk of overinvesting. For example, you can estimate if there is sufficient economic potential to fund an extra headcount or even to hire an agency to help out. Remember, though, that such a calculation of a potential personalized future should be taken with a grain of salt. It's not fortune telling, but nor is it an exact science. See it as decision support.

When calculating the true monetary uplift, remember that for marketing automation flows and personalization of content feeds on inbound platforms, the reasonable period for measuring return on investment (ROI) is quite long when compared to campaigns. This is due to the automated nature of the process and the relatively small need to update content and flows once they're up and running. Eventually these projects will have a much higher ROI than most manual campaigns when the one-time effort they require is taken into consideration over time.

MATURITY LEVELS FOR A PERSONALIZED CUSTOMER EXPERIENCE – THE PYRAMID OF PERSONALIZATION

Throughout *Part II* of the book we have deconstructed personalization into the constituent insights and content elements of the Bowtie of Personalization. We have also described how you can use the bowtie to look more clearly at value creation from personalization within the three major marketing disciplines: campaigns, marketing automation, and inbound platforms.

We have conceptualized three levels of maturity for each of these disciplines. The three levels all contain 'scopes' – in other words, types of communication you build when working with personalization. As you may already have noticed, the closer you get to the top level of maturity, the more centralized and channel agnostic the scope becomes. This is why we use the term 'pyramid': because the disciplines come together at the peak, the model begins to resemble a pyramid. All three disciplines gradually move towards centralized management of content, AI-based insights, and matching of these insights with content. We also see a movement towards catering more to a good customer experience as opposed to pushing short-term sales, and thus creating and preserving long-term value. In the end, the result is true personalized omnichannel marketing.

What we've covered in *Part II* constitutes the **front end** of the pyramid. This is where effectiveness is born. Becoming efficient is another matter. How do you build a team and an organization that can work efficiently with personalization? This is what we will explore in *Part IV* of the book, where we describe the **back end** of the pyramid.

The three levels of maturity will give you a chance to evaluate your own company's maturity and how far you've come. *Figure 17* provides a simplified overview of the maturity levels for all three disciplines.

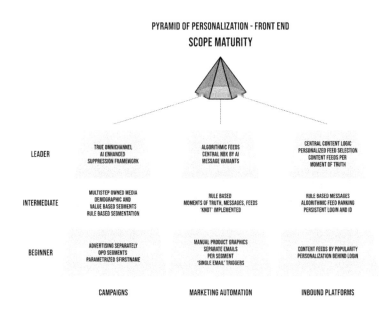

Figure 17. The front end of the Pyramid of Personalization.

We realize that the cases where companies have organized themselves to support omnichannel personalization across the customer journey and truly match insights with content for all customers are few and far between. When this happens, however, it opens up the possibility of creating truly memorable personalized experiences across channels. Mixing the somewhat technical part of personalization with a bit of creativity and warmth truly holds the potential for putting 'the person back in personalization', as our fellow personalization author David Mannheim's argues in his new book.[4]

Achieving this kind of maturity within personalization both allows for and requires a whole other way of working. It needs a new operating model, as we shall discuss later when we look at the back end of the pyramid in *Part IV*.

But first, we need to deliver on our promise to explore the possibility that personalization might *not* be the answer or the right tactic. Is personalization a good tactic for any digital project? Any business challenge? Any business sector? In the next part of the book, we shall explore these very questions.

PART THREE
THE PREREQUISITES FOR PERSONALIZATION

CHAPTER 15
THE BASIC FOUNDATIONS
FOR PERSONALIZATION

Encountering all the exciting opportunities for using personalization to drive extra value in campaigns, marketing automation, and platform projects, it is easy to get the feeling that personalization must be for everyone. It's not, however. Personalization, as we defined it in *Chapter 3*, is a distinct communication tactic – it is not the *only* communication tactic. So, if it's not a given that personalization is always a good thing to do, it's important to explore those scenarios where it isn't.

In this chapter and the next two, we'll explore various topics related to the following two questions:

1. Could you do it?
2. Is it the right thing to do (now)?

The first question relates to whether your organization can tick the boxes required to actually make personalization happen – in other words, do you have the necessary prerequisites? The second question relates more to the timing of doubling down on personalization: is now the right time for your business, given the challenges you are currently facing?

THREE AREAS TO MANAGE WELL BEFORE INVESTING IN PERSONALIZATION

When we discussed the notion of marketing without personalization in *Chapter 5*, we also looked at a key prerequisite for personalization – namely, the value proposition. If your general value proposition is not in place, then you don't have product–market fit and personalization will help you very little. Superficial scratches in the core customer experience can, to some extent, be fixed by timely and relevant communication. However, if your value proposition is not in place, then we strongly suggest not investing in personalization yet.

Even if your value proposition is in place, there are still some fundamental areas to manage well before doubling down on personalization as the winning strategy, as shown in *Figure 18*. The remainder of this chapter explores these three essentials.

Figure 18. Personalization requires that your core offering is in place, you have established brand trust and demand, and you have access to plentiful customer data.

SOLID CORE OFFERING

Consider your company's whole value chain, all the way from having the right suppliers to delivering service on a good product. How well oiled are those processes? Is your sales process working? Are your prices competitive? Are your website and (where relevant) your ecommerce driving conversions? Do you have the right payment options in place for the various markets to which you sell? How is your last-mile delivery system?

If the answer to one of more of these questions is 'well, not so good', then personalization may not be for you (yet).

BRAND TRUST AND DEMAND

The second thing to ask yourself is whether or not your brand has managed to establish trust with consumers. Having an unknown brand would obviously mean you'd have to answer that question with a resounding 'no'. Therefore, if no one knows about you, then we suggest you first work more on your brand and how it is perceived, and ultimately create demand and traffic to your sales channels.

Once you have created brand trust and there is a demand for your offerings, your sales efforts and ultimately your personalization efforts will pay off to a much greater extent. According to Qualtrics, 63% of surveyed consumers responded that a company's reputation affected their purchasing decisions.[1] This isn't that weird when you think about it. Think about how you interact with brands and how you interact with other people – it's not that different. Just as you'd be unlikely to buy a used car (or anything) from a person who was unknown to you or who appeared dodgy, you'd be unlikely to buy from a company with no or poor reviews. And then imagine if the person or the company somehow knew all about you. How would you feel about them addressing personal topics with you? Creeped out, most likely!

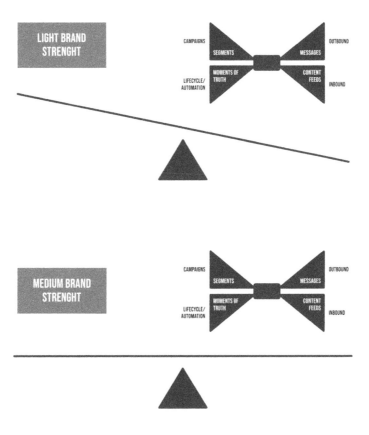

Figure 19. A strong brand brings great leverage to your personalization efforts; before brand strength is created, personalization makes little difference.

Budgets should be allocated to both advertising and delivering good experiences, and on getting those experiences documented in credible reviews that are easily accessible by consumers who wish to evaluate your brand.

ACCESS TO PLENTIFUL CUSTOMER DATA

Throughout this book, we haven't exactly kept it a secret that you need customer data to provide the insights needed for personalization. Customer data – and a lot of it – is the single most important prerequisite. However, companies have varying degrees of access to customer data depending on their go-to-market model (see *Figure 20*). Companies in fast-moving consumer goods (FMCG) have a much harder time collecting customer data than their digital direct-to-consumer peers.

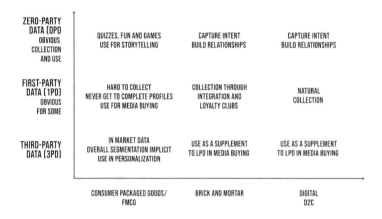

Figure 20. Brands from different industries have varying opportunities for collecting and using customer data (see definitions of zero-party (ZPD), first-party (1PD), and third-party (3PD) data in the paragraph on 'data types' below).

If you are not selling directly to customers but instead through resellers or marketplaces such as Amazon, Miinto, or Zalando, then you'll most likely have very little customer data or so-called first-party data. This will be the case for most manufacturers of consumer packaged goods and FMCG.

Classic brick-and-mortar retailers will have an easier time gathering first-party data than resellers will, but they will often have to launch some kind of loyalty club in order to collect transactional data on a personal level in their physical stores. Business-to-business models have the advantage here in that most purchases will be linked to an identifiable customer that gets an invoice at the end of each month.

Digital companies working directly with customers – whether business-to-consumer or business-to-business – are best positioned when it comes to collecting customer data. This category of companies naturally includes the new breed of online entertainment companies (e.g. Netflix and Spotify), but more traditional companies have also moved into this space. It's hard to run a bank, an insurance company, or even most travel agencies today without collecting a lot of customer data. However, the incumbents of these industries often suffer from legacy systems and data that is hard to integrate or even dig out for marketing purposes. Thus, having a lot of customer data isn't always a blessing.

DATA TYPES

We have mentioned first-party data (1PD) and third-party data (3PD) several times now, so a little introduction to these data types is probably long overdue.

First-party data is the data that your company collects directly from customers. It is typically gathered from transactions, subscriptions, wish-lists, and other behavioural data (e.g. from your app, website, or ecommerce solution).

If someone collects this data and sells it to you, then it becomes second-party data (2PD). Before you use this data, make sure that the consents used to collect it enable you to use it lawfully. Second-party data is probably the category of data that companies use the least.

Third-party data is data that is publicly available and not necessarily linked directly to your customers or business. Often this is data of a more contextual nature. Data in this category might include the weather forecast, records within a licence plate registry, today's TV programmes, Mosaic or Conzoom profiles for households (addresses), statistical information on land plots, or the in-market behaviour or segmentation criteria you can use when you are purchasing advertising.

In 2018, the term 'zero-party data' (ZPD) saw the light of day for the first time.[2] This is data that is submitted in, for example, surveys or on 'My profile' pages. At first glance, the category might seem a bit unnecessary, as this data has been a vital part of permissions marketing since the beginning. Prior to 2022, it was always called and treated as first-party data. However, due to the fact that this data isn't integrated with other sources or automatically updated, it starts to lose its value as soon as it has been created. For example, if a customer has informed you that she has *one* child, how often do you then need to re-ask this question to be sure you can count on the data? The same goes for job titles, marital statuses, addresses, and so on. In this way, you can argue that zero-party data is data that you 'borrow' from the customer. The extra category therefore helps you to distinguish it from behavioural first-party data (e.g. transactions and purchases within the last month).

SPECIAL CONSIDERATIONS FOR FMCG

If we think about the Bowtie of Personalization and then consider the options for FMCG companies when working with personalization, it is pretty clear that these businesses face a much bigger challenge and quite limited options when working with personalization. For a start, they have very little first-party data since their resellers are the ones who own the transactions. So, they are left with third-party data or the in-market behavioural data they can access when buying exposure on paid media. This makes it almost impossible for them to do any marketing automation since they'll be lacking the data to build any insights in the form of moments of truth.

On the content side of things, they do, of course, have products. However, advertising from an FMCG point of view is most often executed as a top-funnel branding exercise, leaving the resellers to do the tactical marketing campaigns. Top-funnel branding is more about telling the story of the brand than it is about selling products through promotions and offers. So, taking these two things into account, it's clear that FMCG companies are pretty much stuck in the upper part of the bowtie (see *Figure 21*).

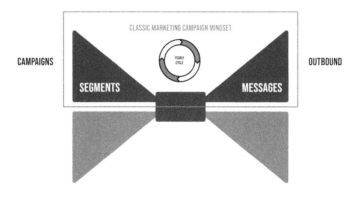

Figure 21. Classic FMCG is stuck in the upper part of the Bowtie of Personalization.

Naturally, there are also FMCG companies that sell directly to customers, and this allows them to collect first-party data to some extent. However, the volume of their direct selling is rarely comparable to the volume that their resellers deal with. So, in terms of the money that can be made from using this data to personalize communication for the relatively small audience reachable through owned media, this is hardly worth the effort. On paid media, though, a small sample of first-party data can definitely be useful when buying media and searching for lookalike audiences for first-party data segments.

VALUE PROPOSITIONS WITH FREQUENT ENGAGEMENT CREATE MORE AND BETTER DATA

It's not only the go-to-market model that matters when you are collecting data. Some products are needed more often than others and thus create more frequent transactions and data points. How often do people buy a broom, for instance? And there's also the matter of how much people care about certain products. Again, a broom matters little to most people. It could, however, be part of a larger assortment of cleaning products that has a specific audience if treated as a joint value proposition.

As an example, Nestlé brings a wide array of products to market in the Nordics. Some of these have very little potential to gather data – KitKat, for instance. This is a very strong brand, however, it is also low involvement and therefore challenging to get data from the consumers. For most people it will not take up much headspace that they should remember to buy KitKat – on the contrary – the decision to buy a KitKat emerges in the store and often when the KitKat is on a special offer. At best, consumers might be convinced to join fun games and sweepstakes and thus engage deeper with the brand – but it's hardly getting to any serious body of zero-person or first-person data any time soon. At the other end of the scale, Nestlé has Purina pet food. If there's one thing that people care a lot about then it's their pets – their mental wellbeing, how healthy they are, how their fur looks, and so on. Thus, the Purina brand has a lot of potential for engaging customers and fairly easily creating a lot of data through these interactions. This is a great example of a FMCG product with high involvement.

We've now covered the basic prerequisites for working with personalization. If your core offering isn't in place and your brand is nowhere – needless to say, these issues need attention before you double down on personalization as the big thing. It's also worth taking a look at your value proposition and your go-to-market model. Do these support the collection of enough first-party data to support meaningful personalization? And to what extent? Looking back at the Bowtie of Personalization, it's clear that without any behavioural data, you'll never unlock personalization that relies on the bottom part of the bowtie.

It's one thing to have the *opportunity* to get a lot of first-party data. It's another to actually have it. And then comes the question of quality. The next chapter goes into more detail about the kinds of things you need to consider to ensure your data can support personalization.

CHAPTER 16
DATA AND PERSONALIZATION

The previous chapter explained how access to first-party data is an essential prerequisite for personalization – at least, if you can't settle for personalizing your campaigns only. But there are various other aspects that you need to consider relating to data and personalization. This chapter explores data cleanliness, how much data is needed, and how to scale permissions and data.

IS YOUR DATA CLEAN?

Having a lot of data is a good step towards profitable personalization – it won't get you all the way, though. As discussed in the previous chapter, zero-party data can easily become outdated, so it has to be somewhat recent in order for it to do the job.

But this is by no means the only potential issue with data. It could also be that you have many duplicates in your database where the same individual is registered multiple times, for example with the same email address. You don't want to be sending the same information multiple times to the same individual. So, these need to be cleaned up. It could also be that your contact information is disconnected in the sense that you may have separate lists for email addresses and phone numbers, meaning that you don't know which emails and numbers are for the same individuals. If you want to create seamless customer journeys, you need to be able to identify a customer no matter which channel you meet them on.

Another common data flaw relates to the use of country codes with mobile phone numbers. Do you have a country code for all individuals? Should phone numbers have 00 or + first? Can your marketing automation platform or execution engine handle this? Most likely this will need to be fixed further down in your marketing technology stack (see *Chapter 20*).

HOW MUCH DATA IS NEEDED TO MAKE PERSONALIZATION PROFITABLE?

Within farming, the effect of adding fertilizer to the soil in order to boost yield is measured using a model called the MRTN (maximum return to nitrogen) curve.[1] The curve shows that at a certain point the extra yield generated by adding more fertilizer is not worth the additional fertilizer cost.

Within personalization, there's a similar curve (see *Figure 22*). Imagine that the scale of your customer database and/or website traffic is equivalent to the size of a farm's fields, and then imagine that personalization is the fertilizer that will bring you a higher yield. The fertilizer comes at a cost – namely, the resources needed to produce personalized campaigns and marketing automation flows and to optimize personalized content feeds. The more land you have (i.e. the bigger your database or the more website traffic you have), the more you can justify investing in fertilizer because you can expect the extra yield to bring you more money than you invested in the fertilizer. On the other hand, this also means that there's always an inflection point where you should stop investing in personalization.

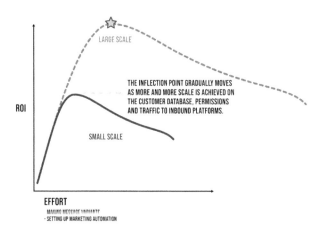

Figure 22. The additional effect of personalization is highly dependent on the scale of your database: the larger the database, the more you can justify investing in personalization.

So, how much data is enough to start using personalization? Well, the annoying answer is, of course, that it depends. What is most important is that the amount of data should at least enable your personalization to provide additional earnings to pay for the salaries of the people involved in creating the personalized customer experience. So, if you are a high-end retailer with a database containing marketing permissions for more than a million customers and you have a loyalty club that is used often by your customers, you should be good to go. That would place your company in the upper right part of the model in *Figure 23*.

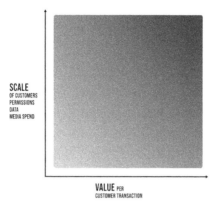

SCALE
OF CUSTOMERS
PERMISSIONS
DATA
MEDIA SPEND

VALUE PER
CUSTOMER TRANSACTION

Figure 23. The combination of Scale of your database and Value per transaction is a determining factor for deciding if personalization is profitable.

The smaller your scale, however, the smaller the potential returns. Compared to the retailer with over a million customers, a pure-play ecommerce website with 5,000 known customers and permissions will have a much lower limit for how much should be invested in personalization. In the matrix in *Figure 23*, this company would be placed in the lower left quadrant.

Cost-effective personalization for this company could be achieved through, for example, built-in personalization of on-site product feeds (provided that the ecommerce system supports it – or there might be an easy implementation of an external system). Or it could take the form of simple segmentation of the database for outbound campaigns (such as by gender or by primary interest in categories – all depending on the assortment, of course). One final possibility would be to use some sort of bottom-funnel cart-abandonment tactic, such as an email when a basket is abandoned, or the simplest lookalike audience marketing on paid media.

If, however, the value of a transaction in your business is very high, this can make up for a lack of scale. If the same ecommerce business were selling high-end luxury products or if it were a business-to-business company selling windmills or other similar products, then 5,000 known customers and permissions could be considered sufficient to make deeper personalization worth the effort. Then the company would fall within the lower right quadrant of *Figure 23*.

Having a large-scale customer database with permissions and transactions alongside a high value per customer (upper right quadrant of *Figure 23*) is, of course, the dream scenario and personalization should be a no-brainer. On the other hand, if scale is big but customer value is low (upper left quadrant), then personalization could, for instance, be used to try to improve customers' purchasing frequency and gradually move them towards buying higher-margin products (e.g. like private-label products would normally have). Most likely it will be your industry and/or core value proposition that has the strongest effect on your value per customer, though.

RE-EVALUATE OFTEN!

Having enough data is a moving target! If the scale of your company's customers, permissions, and data are on the low side, and if your core value proposition is both highly engaging and involving, then it will only be a matter of time before personalization becomes a reasonable investment. This is time that you should spend chasing new customers and their permissions – and, of course, the first transaction with each of these customers. So put deep personalization efforts on hold until you've achieved scale with your customers, permissions, and first-party data.

HOW TO SCALE PERMISSIONS AND DATA

The most important thing to do in order to scale permissions and data is to keep asking customers for consent no matter where you meet them. If you have a massive retail presence in brick-and-mortar stores, then train and incentivize your sales associates to always ask for loyalty club membership. Use gamification software on your website and in your app to always ask unknown visitors for marketing consent and let them submit a little profile data through fun and engaging games. And, of course, use 'lead ads' when you are advertising on social media to give you new marketing consents directly from your advertising.

You should also consider sending out automated emails with the sole purpose of engaging customers and getting them to submit more data (or update old data) about themselves. Do a monthly prize draw for customers with a 'full profile' or use the GDPR (General Data Protection Regulation) as an excuse to ask people to kindly update their information. Simply displaying their information directly within an email can lower the threshold for getting them to engage. Seeing outdated information about oneself is a good nudge towards updating it.

As an example of chasing more marketing permissions, the Danish kitchenware retailer Kop & Kande boosted its permissions base by approximately 15,000 new permissions through a fairly simple Christmas Advent calendar on its homepage. Everything was done with 'no code configuration' and in collaboration with the company's suppliers.[2]

The Danish retailer COOP has taken this one step further. According to the company's Commercial Director, Peter Boris Kreilgaard, COOP is now selling similar gamification campaigns to its suppliers as 'retail media' (as described in *Chapter 9*).[3]

PERSISTENT CUSTOMER LOG-INS

One way to collect more behavioural data from your website and app is to entice customers to create a profile and to log in. And make sure that the log-in is persistent, so that users don't have to log in over and over again. Customers can be enticed to log in by offering functionality that is solely available for logged-in users. This could take the form of personalized product feeds with favourites or previously bought products, as in the case of the grocery etailer Nemlig.com, discussed in *Chapter 12*. It could also include previously visited products or products that the customer had in their basket earlier.

With a recent initiative, Amazon Style, Amazon has even made it possible to visit one of the company's physical locations, scan products, and add them to 'your fitting room'. As customers browse the physical products in the store, they can choose to scan barcodes on products they wish to try on (already being logged in on the app, obviously). These products will then not only appear in the fitting room but also remain as a data point long after the session is over.

We've now covered what the scale of your customer database, your marketing permissions, and your first-party data means for the results you can potentially create through personalization. The next chapter considers one final topic related to prerequisites for personalization, namely conversion rate optimization (CRO), and then offers some conclusions on when you should and shouldn't consider personalization.

CHAPTER 17
CONVERSION RATE OPTIMIZATION AND PERSONALIZATION

The previous chapter showed how your decision to personalize (or not) should be closely linked to the current scale of your customer database. If you've decided you need to build more scale, there are options for your marketing team beyond waiting around for scale to build. How about conversion rate optimization (CRO)?

CRO and personalization are two very different things. Quite often, however, you'll find the same people discussing and even working with them. CRO is a discipline that relates closely to ecommerce and is all about removing friction for users who are potentially wanting to make a purchase with you. It's about experimenting to find the best possible selection and positioning of content, navigation, and functionality to maximize the share of visitors who convert to become customers by making a purchase.

PRIORITIZING BETWEEN CRO AND PERSONALIZATION

On most websites – and especially if you haven't applied the data collection tactics mentioned in the previous chapter – many or even most visitors will be anonymous. The only thing identifying a visitor will be the session cookie, which is living an increasingly short life due to the tech giants carefully crafting their own walled gardens of data in the name of privacy (i.e. they are killing the cookie and spoiling email-open-rate tracking).[1]

So, if the majority of your visitors are anonymous, it makes sense to retain a heavy focus on optimizing the general customer experience on your website. And even if you can identify most of your visitors, you'll still want to spend plenty of time on optimization, simply because building websites, ecommerce platforms, and apps is complex. Many arbitrary design decisions are made during such a project and thus there is very little chance that you will get them all right on the first go (no matter how good your personas and your designers are).

SHIFTING FROM CRO TOWARDS PERSONALIZATION

For most marketing projects, then, it makes sense to optimize for your unknown customers until you have got to know them. Once you know them well enough and you've removed most of the friction from the generic experience, you can switch to personalization tactics instead – while still measuring the effect in much the same way as with CRO. In practice, if possible, always test the personalized version (i.e. all the personalized variants as a whole) against a non-personalized version. Essentially, you're still doing CRO – but with personalization on top. Refer back to *Chapter 14* for a recap on measuring the value from personalization.

WHEN TO SHIFT FROM CRO TO PERSONALIZATION

Due to the differing nature of marketing projects, the best time to switch from a CRO approach to a personalization approach will vary. Think back to our discussion in *Chapter 8* about how important the message is when working with inbound versus outbound communication. The message is by far the most important aspect when working outbound. As a consequence, personalization should start earlier for this type of marketing. Let's explore this point a little more deeply, stepping through each of the scenarios summarized in *Figure 24*.

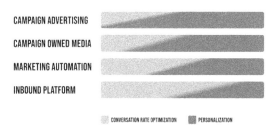

CAMPAIGN ADVERTISING

CAMPAIGN OWNED MEDIA

MARKETING AUTOMATION

INBOUND PLATFORM

CONVERSATION RATE OPTIMIZATION   PERSONALIZATION

Figure 24. The moment to switch from optimizing the general experience to personalizing the specific experience varies between the marketing disciplines.

Following our fairly wide definition of personalization (see *Chapter 3*), working with campaigns on paid media is hardly possible without doing some kind of personalization. Gone are the days when everybody watched the same TV show on Friday night. The closest modern equivalent we can come up with is the Superbowl in the USA. So many people watch this that in practice very little personalization (or in this case, segmentation) takes place. Even if we turn to out-of-home media such as posters on bus stops or billboards, the choice of placement will be determined based on the kind of people living in each neighbourhood.

For campaigns based on owned media, such as email newsletters, there is definitely the option of sending a one-size-fits-all newsletter, and we all receive these now and again. Many marketers are doing subject line testing, which is basically CRO. On the other hand, it takes very little effort to let customers self-segment – either at sign-up (by clicking 'Subscribe to women's' or 'Subscribe to men's') or by asking for a few details (such as interests or preferences). So, even if you have trouble getting data integrated into your execution platforms, there is almost no excuse not to do a little personalization of at least the subject line, the highlighted offer, or the selection of product feeds in the emails themselves. The point is that personalization starts early for owned media campaigns.

Marketing automation projects focus primarily on matching the right moment of truth with the right message. As long as this message is generic and supports the customer in completing a certain task by removing friction, you could argue that it is in fact both CRO *and* personalization. When the time comes to craft specific variants of this message depending on the receiving segments, however, you've definitely moved on to personalization.

As discussed earlier in this chapter, the switch to personalization from CRO comes late for many inbound platform projects, such as websites and apps. On these platforms, the personalization of messages is secondary to personalizing the content feeds for products, articles, shows, and such. Nevertheless, to the extent that it is easy to personalize your content feeds, then by all means start this process early. But hold back on your effort to personalize messages and functionality for a while.

Die-hard CRO fans will argue that increasing conversions by 1% for 100% of visitors using CRO is as good as increasing conversions by 10% for 10% of visitors using personalization. Based on a firm belief in the long-term effect of personalization on customer loyalty and emotional commitment, we would argue that customers who have a seriously personalized experience will also have had a much more memorable experience that stands out, stays in their memory, and is worth telling their friends about. Personalization runs deeper than just chasing conversions.

SO, WHO IS PERSONALIZATION *NOT* FOR?

In this part of the book, we set out to discuss when personalization is *not* the right communication tactic. To conclude on this topic, first of all, we strongly suggest only doubling down on personalization if your basic value proposition is in place and your core business is working properly. If this is not the case, then definitely hold back for a while when it comes to personalization. The hype can still be real (see *Chapter 1*) without it necessarily being a good idea for you right now!

Second, you need to have established a trusted brand and created demand for your offering. This may be a marketing exercise, but not one that has a lot to do with personalization. If no one knows your name, you have to start the conversation yourself. And the beginning of that conversation will hardly be personalized. It's about who you are and what you deliver. The *Marketing Week* article we discussed in *Chapter 2* about forgetting personalization because it 'doesn't work' is about this exact scenario. Of course, you shouldn't have one version of your core brand story for each individual.

Third, customer data is needed to determine the insights that will fuel your personalization. If your go-to-market model makes it too hard to ever achieve scale for known customers and to collect the corresponding first-party data, then personalization will not be the most effective tool in your belt. It may still work to some extent on paid media, but within owned media you're not going to be tying any personalization knots any time soon.

Finally, if you do have the opportunity to collect first-party data and consents from known customers but just haven't achieved scale yet, then it's more a matter of time before personalization is the right communications tactic for you. Spend this time optimizing the core customer experience in its generic form while collecting marketing consents and first-party data.

PART FOUR
ORGANIZATIONAL MATURITY FOR PERSONALIZATION

CHAPTER 18
MODELS OF ORGANIZATIONAL MATURITY IN PERSONALIZATION

Let's assume that having read this far, you have silently nodded along during the description of the Bowtie of Personalization and the exploration of the prerequisites. You have a sound value proposition, a solid core business, brand trust, and plenty of customer data in place. You may even have used the guidance for creating good personalization results within campaigns, marketing automation, and platform projects. And you might have evaluated which level of the Pyramid of Personalization you're at when it comes to the scope of what you've built (i.e. the front end of the pyramid).

But it's one thing knowing what to build and quite another knowing how to take it to the top level while continuing to make it profitable. As we shall see in this chapter on moving up through the maturity levels in personalization, there are definitely organizational matters that you will need to address and glass ceilings you will need to break through. If you do not, you will miss out on great value.

In this chapter, we'll explore the back end of the Pyramid of Personalization, which as we will see consists of three focus areas, each with three maturity levels. The back end enables the front end. We'll explain how we found inspiration for the model and dive deep into the three main focus areas and what constitutes maturity within each one.

THE OMNICHANNEL HEXAGON

Rasmus Houlind and Colin Shearer's book *Make It All About Me* introduced a three-step maturity model called the Omnichannel Hexagon (see *Figure 25*).[1] This model spans six disciplines and it can support various departments, job roles, and functions in becoming more customer-centric. One of the key points in the book is that organizations don't abandon the tasks in the outer layers of the hexagon as they progress towards the centre. For instance, the authors suggest that organizations continue to work on broad campaigns to attract new customers in tandem with one-to-one personalization for well-known and engaged customers. Companies will most likely also still be doing segmented communication based on simple data points even if advanced insights built by AI are also available.

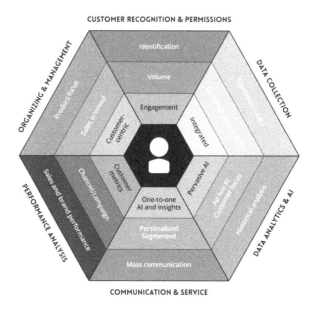

Figure 25. The Omnichannel Hexagon: a maturity model for evaluating omnichannel marketing maturity.

The Omnichannel Hexagon, however, is not so detailed on:

1. The different elements that make up personalization
2. The software needed to support major use cases
3. How to progress from each level to the next

We have already covered item one in this book. However, we still haven't really touched on the software or on the question of how to progress to the most mature level. With the help of the back end of the Pyramid of Personalization, this part of the book will address these points in detail.

A REALISTIC VIEW ON ORGANIZATIONAL MATURITY WITHIN PERSONALIZATION

We sought further inspiration in the work of Forrester Consulting. They included a balanced method of assessing organizational maturity in a study from 2022 on the European state of omnichannel marketing automation.[2] Respondent organizations were measured across six dimensions (see also *Figure 26*):

1. Strategy
2. People, culture, and skills
3. Process
4. Measurement
5. Technology
6. Data

Figure 26. The omnichannel marketing maturity assessment by Forrester Consulting.

The study reveals how people-related challenges (such as 'aligning between data/insights and marketing teams' or 'lacking the right talent') can prove to be equally as challenging as tech challenges (such as the 37% of the respondents who 'lack the sophisticated operational tools' or the 32% who 'lack a martech roadmap') when trying to get the best results. In this way, it does touch upon some of the elements within both software and governance that we seek to address. However, the model doesn't offer any view on how to work with any of these challenges.

PRODUCTIZATION IN MARKETING

Perhaps our most important source of inspiration for the back end of the Pyramid of Personalization is the model of marketing productization created by our co-author Frans Riemersma of MartechTribe (see *Best-of*).[3] This is a means of gauging how well marketing processes and thus governance are capable of evolving in maturity over time. To achieve the highest level of personalized customer experience that we envisioned in the front end of the Pyramid of Personalization, your organization needs to get to a place where you almost treat personalization as if it were a product in its own right. Getting to this level requires a transition from focusing on projects to focusing on the process.

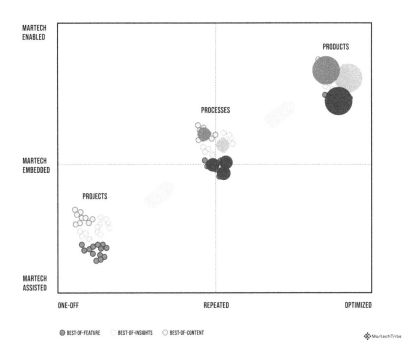

Figure 27. Productizing marketing.

In seemingly perfect harmony with the Bowtie of Personalization, the 'atoms' of each level of the MartechTribe model consist of three core elements: content, insights, and the new kid in class, features. You as a marketer need to know what drives each customer journey to the next level. You need to know what content and insights drive value together. To do this, you need data to get closer to the moments of truth. But you also need software with features because insights and content do not deliver personalization results automatically. Content and data live in software. Software then allows you to combine both content and insights and thus personalize.

Instead of relying on data and technology to solve problems by themselves, you should experiment at each level. The goal is to find out what the few main insights, content assets, and core features are that, when combined, drive conversions and value. These experiments all have a start and an end date, much like projects or the campaigns you are running already. Over time you will see patterns or common denominators across the projects.

You will be able to extract a rule from each of the experiments and design a standard. Defining a standard essentially means ruling out the exceptions. Exceptions cannot (and should not) be automated, and everything that is standardized can be automated via processes. Automation is another word for productization.

The idea of defining, standardizing, and automating is to produce repeatable and predictable personalized customer experiences that benefit both the company and the customer. Products are not necessarily saleable items with a price tag attached to them so that they can be sold to customers. Products can also be internal or operational, such as microservices, integrations, or reports. Just as many organizations have a 'product owner' for a process or an output, you can appoint a product owner for a specific track of your marketing (e.g. weekly newsletters) or for a specific part of the customer journey (e.g. the 'win-back journey'). However, the goal of productization is zero maintenance. As you can see from the growing dark bubbles in *Figure 27*, at every stage you are using more marketing technology (martech) and as you continue this trend, fewer human resources are needed. Product owners ensure that 'products' will free up resources so that the team can now run new experiments as opposed to running the old manual tasks.

The three maturity stages of this process require you to develop three versions of your 'personalization product', as follows:

1. **Hack** – The purpose of this version is to find 'hacks' (shortcuts) to growth. All that is important is to pull the insights and content together in features with one goal: to see whether each combination is viable. This is essentially rapid prototyping. The point is to create initial traction with real-life customers. Therefore, the Hack version lives outside your standardized technology, insight, and content ecosystem.
2. **Pack** – Once the Hack version has generated enough traction, you are ready for the Pack version of your personalization product. As experiments come with many variations, you'll end up with a lot of unnecessary content, insights, features, and integrations. The idea is now to leave out all that is redundant

and be left with the core essence of the ideal customer experience. The goal is to create a lean and mean version of the Hack version.

3. **Stack** – The cleaned-up Pack version is now ready for integration into your platform ecosystem. The goal is zero maintenance. Only then can you free up your efforts and your resources.

Between each of the three stages, there is a glass ceiling that you will need to break through.

THE BACK END OF THE PYRAMID OF PERSONALIZATION

Because of the high correlation between the productification of marketing approach and what we set out to achieve with the Pyramid of Personalization, we have chosen to adopt the above three overall maturity levels for the back end of the pyramid (see *Figure 28*). But what are the underlying components? Naturally, it's all about insights, content, and software – but how do you get the skills needed to get those insights, produce that content, and operate the software? What does good look like for this journey? And what challenges will you most likely encounter along the way?

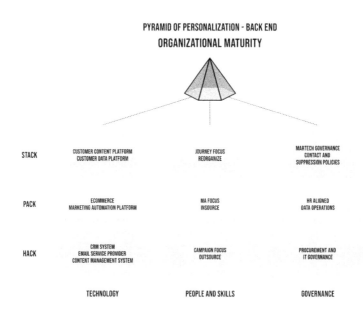

Figure 28. The back end of the Pyramid of Personalization: how to organize optimally for personalization.

Matching your customer insights with your content is the core of personalization, as this book has argued. But it takes a great degree of skill and considerable resources to achieve this match and actually execute personalized marketing in a productified manner. These skills must be both creative and technical. And when it comes to technical skills, these are a necessity today since almost all marketing is done from some kind of software platform. The term 'marketing technologist' refers to the tech-savvy marketer who is adept at using technologies and software across the board. A marketing team will consist of several such marketing technologists, each with their areas of expertise. We'd argue that the use of technology and the way you tie the knot in the bowtie can definitely also be done in creative ways.

The selection of software to help the teams execute naturally also plays a role. There is no shortage of software vendors, but this also means that it can be extremely difficult to choose the right software platforms – from the points of view of both getting the job done and choosing the systems that will best fit together in the 'stack'.

A martech stack is a selection of marketing software tools that support the operations of a full marketing team across marketing disciplines. Quite often, the functionality of the tools overlap, so important decisions need to be made about who works in which system to carry out which task. Often there isn't a perfect solution or combination, and one task could potentially be carried out equally well in multiple systems. For large enterprise organizations, this is especially complex as different divisions might not even be aware of the tools used in other parts of the organization. This is where governance comes in – the topic of *Chapter 21*. Governance within marketing and personalization is all about how you organize and manage processes concerning both software and skills so as to comply with external legal requirements and internal company regulations. It is also about imposing your own internal governance to help drive your marketing success in a sustainable way and thus increase your maturity.

In the final few chapters of this book, we'll explore how skills, software, and governance develop over the three organizational maturity levels in the back end of the Pyramid of Personalization. How do the Hack, Pack, and Stack levels look in greater detail? *Figure 28* gave you a glimpse via a simplified overview, and the following chapters will go into further depth.

CHAPTER 19
PEOPLE AND SKILLS FOR PERSONALIZATION

Pernille felt as if the Royal Danish Theatre was ready to take its marketing efforts up a notch. The team had a fairly well-functioning ecommerce website that highlighted upcoming shows and allowed for the purchase of both tickets and season passes. Their digital campaign offering was also working pretty well, both in terms of advertising and in terms of email marketing. They'd even implemented a marketing automation platform with several automated communication flows that helped to fill the seats at the theatre's four locations. And last but not least, their app was effective at providing practical information and enabling refreshments to be ordered. At the level of each channel, things were going well, but they still had to sell more tickets to meet their budgets. The question was, where could they drive the extra sales at the lowest cost?

They weren't exactly done with telling new people about the wonders of the Royal Danish Theatre. However, the sheer size of their existing customer database told Pernille that there was still great potential to drive frequency and ultimately sell more season passes to previous guests who were already in the database. Luckily, she'd been able to relay the understanding of this commercial potential internally and had received approval for an extra headcount. Now she was ready to start recruiting.

Being the marketing director didn't mean that she was in control of all marketing-related resources. Her rather small team relied on others, such as the colleagues who provided the insights from the theatre's customer data as well as the colleagues in charge of the app. The team also used agencies from time to time. She was now at a point where she had to decide very carefully which role to recruit for.

Looking at her small team, Pernille had, of course, her webmaster, who was fully occupied with keeping the ecommerce website as frictionless as possible. There was still a lot to optimize relating to the general user experience (UX) on this channel. She also had employees with extremely deep system knowledge of the customer relationship management (CRM) system, ticketing, and marketing automation platform (MAP). However, in her mind, the team could and should spend more time building and executing communication through the same set-up. This did not mean that they should do more of their quite effective multi-wave campaigns, which they were already producing on an ongoing basis. They needed someone with a customer mindset who was technical enough to help make their campaign production more efficient. This would help to free up resources to increase the number of personalized and automated communication flows across channels. It was obvious to Pernille that the team's inclusion of transactional emails had boosted performance. There was no reason they shouldn't continue this approach and involve the app as an outbound communication channel as well as look further into how their first-party data could also increase the efficiency of their advertising.

In the case study above, Pernille is keenly aware that she is in need of more people to help the Royal Danish Theatre reach its goals for ticket sales. Her team have spent a few years establishing their core systems, including an ecommerce-enabled website, an app, and a marketing automation platform. Now it feels as if it's time to stop building more cars and instead take the ones they have for a ride. In other words, it's time to switch gears and start capitalizing on their large investments.

Pernille is by no means alone in realizing that it is no good owning a Formula 1 car if there is no one with the skills and time to drive it. Essentially, the money you spend on software will be wasted if you don't put the software to use. The previous chapter introduced a study by Forrester Consulting on the challenges of succeeding with omnichannel marketing automation.[1] Like many studies before it, this one proved that personalization and marketing automation can have a great impact on business objectives such as growth. The study examined key factors within the areas of people, processes, and technology. Based on their replies, the respondent organizations were divided into beginners, intermediates, and leaders. Not surprisingly, there were a lot of technology-related challenges that came up as standing in the way of organizations progressing up this ranking. More surprisingly, though, it was clear that people challenges were equally if not more important.

The number one challenge mentioned in the study was 'Struggling to understand customer needs and preferences'. It can be argued that this challenge sits right between skills and software, and is closely related to the insights side of the Bowtie of Personalization. Relatedly, the study also mentioned challenges concerning talent, skills, collaboration, internal alignment, and how to leverage third parties in a way that complements a company's internal resources. In a subsequent webinar, personalization and omnichannel leader Stefan Kirkedal from the internationally acclaimed omnichannel beauty and health retailer Matas even made it clear that he saw people challenges as *even more important* than tech challenges.[2]

ENTER THE MARKETING TECHNOLOGIST

But how can you get an overview of the skills that your team needs? Which roles do you require in your team to effectively work with personalization? One of the people who has given this the most thought is Scott Brinker from Chief Martec. Brinker is most famous in the marketing space for having put together the Marketing Technology Landscape. As we touched upon in *Chapter 1*, the volume of marketing tools available has increased dramatically since the landscape was first launched. Brinker has produced a lot of other valuable insights, including in his book *Hacking Marketing*[3] and a follow-up article in *Harvard Business Review* – 'The Rise of the Chief Marketing Technologist'.[4]

The book and the article sent a clear message that marketing could no longer exist without technology. And because of that, a new breed of executive – namely the chief marketing technologist – was needed to ensure that the right software was available with the right skills to put it to use. Since then, Brinker has taken this methodology even further and provided excellent insights into the team that supports the chief marketing technologist in fulfilling this ambition. In his article 'The Many Splendid Varieties of Marketing Technologists in 2020', he offers various perspectives on martech roles.[5] He also illustrates the four archetypes in the model shown in *Figure 29.*

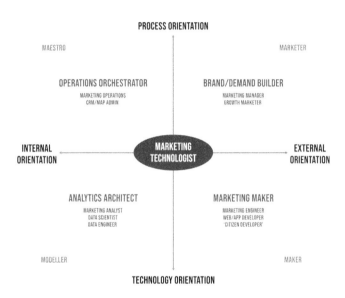

Figure 29. Scott Brinker's four archetypes/roles of marketing technologists.

The model is built on two intersecting axes that make up four quadrants and their respective archetypes. The y-axis has to do with whether the person in question is more concerned with processes or technology (with processes in this case referring to either internal workflows or customer journeys). The x-axis spans from an internal orientation to an external orientation (with external meaning the direction of the customer and marketing that customers will eventually experience as part of their customer journey).

The **Brand/Demand Builders** or **Marketers**, in the top right quadrant, include any marketer who operates technology to produce and implement campaigns and marketing automation flows that drive attention, conversion, and retention of prospects and customers. These people have titles such as digital marketing manager, campaign manager, CRM manager, and marketing automation specialist.

The **Operations Orchestrators** or **Maestros**, in the top left corner, have an internal process focus and thus work with workflows, rules, reports, and tech stacks. They are system admins and marketing operation managers, and they make sure that the processes around systems and data support modelling, execution, and reporting. Their titles include CRM admin, marketing automation platform admin, marketing operations manager, data operations manager, and martech manager.

The **Analytics Architects** or **Modellers**, in the bottom left quadrant, are the people who generate insights from data, diving deep into analytics systems to generate customer and business intelligence. They do this both on an aggregated level and on an individual customer level through the use of algorithms and machine learning. Typical titles include data engineer, data scientist, data analyst, and machine learning engineer.

The **Marketing Makers** or simply **Makers**, in the bottom right quadrant, are the people occupied with building websites, apps, and other platforms that customers either purchase from or use as an integrated part of the customer experience. They are technology oriented, doing their work through either code or low-code applications. Typical titles include web developer, app developer, CMS developer, front end developer, systems integrator, CMS developer, and similar.

Finally, almost like with the Beatles, a fifth **M** is needed to create a full team. This is the **Manager**, who must manage the use of the various skills in the team to support the strategy set by the chief marketing officer or vice president (usually one level further up in the hierarchy). Originally, Brinker called this person the chief marketing technologist (hence his domain ChiefMartec.com), but today this person would be called a customer experience manager, a journey manager, or even a product owner. The last two would apply in situations or at maturity levels where the focus of the team has shifted from optimizing a single channel or marketing discipline towards working channel agnostically on one specific part of the full customer journey.

HOW ABOUT THE CREATIVE SKILLS?

Growth hacking, configuration, and data science can, of course, be considered creative. However, there are also the classic non-technical skills of graphic design, copywriting, and conceptualization at various strategic levels. How do they fit into the 5M model?, you might ask. First, it's a valid point that even though more and more people are using technology that would potentially put them in the Marketer (top right) quadrant, some do indeed work outside marketing technology. Obviously, it would be inappropriate to label these workers as marketing technologists. As Brinker visualizes it, these are part of the broader marketing organization.[6]

HOW THE 5M MODEL APPLIES TO PERSONALIZATION

As *Part III* outlined, there are certain prerequisites that need to be in place before personalization becomes the next obvious move from a business point of view. Obviously, the core business needs to work and the brand must be known and trusted. On top of this, platforms need to be in place and customer data must be plentiful and clean. If we revisit Brinker's 5M model with this mindset, it becomes clear that to begin with, and in order for these prerequisites to be met, there is a much greater need for Maestros and Makers than for Marketers and Modellers (see *Figure 30*). This is not to say that customer insights are not important when designing a website. However, often these insights are of a more qualitative nature and are obtained through anthropological studies and user-centred design, and not necessarily updated on an ongoing basis in a set process.

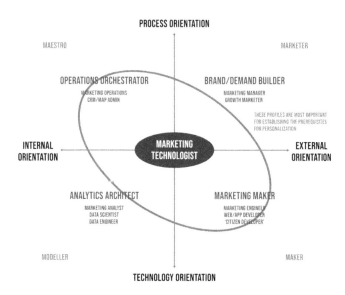

Figure 30. Skills needed to build the foundation for personalization are
mainly from the Maestro and the Maker archetypes.

Once the content management system (CMS), the marketing automation
platform, and potentially the CRM system have been deployed and integrated by the Makers, and data processes have been put in place by the
Maestros, there's a shift in terms of which team is needed. You need to
switch from having a team of builders to having a team of executors – in
other words, rotate out the Maestros and Makers and rotate in the
Modellers and Marketers (see *Figure 31*).

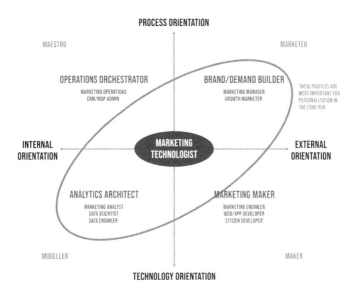

Figure 31. Skills needed to execute personalized marketing from an already existing foundation are mainly from the Marketer and Modeller archetypes.

As you might already have gathered, it turns out that the combined skills of Marketers and Modellers resemble the content of the Bowtie of Personalization. The Modellers work on the insights and the Marketers work on the content as well as the orchestration thereof.

APPLYING THESE SKILLS TO THE PYRAMID OF PERSONALIZATION

These marketing skills can be related to the levels in the Pyramid of Personalization (see *Chapter 18*). As you move up the pyramid, you should shift how your team of marketing technologists is made up as well as how they work.

SHIFTS IN FOCUS

To begin with, when your organizational maturity is at the Hack level of the back end of the Pyramid of Personalization, a fair part of your marketing team should be occupied with establishing your main platforms, such as a website, an ecommerce platform, and potentially an app. In the meantime, your campaign team will be driving traffic and conversions while building up scale in your customer database. The actual campaigns will be at a fairly simple level and not very personalized.

At the Pack level, the main platforms will be in place and thus you should switch towards an execution focus. You will still be driving campaigns but with an increased focus on repeatability and marketing automation. Ultimately and at the Stack level, your team will evolve from having an execution focus to having a channel-agnostic customer journey focus.

SHIFTS IN COMPOSITION

These shifts in focus will have direct impacts on the composition of your team. As we have already mentioned, as you move up the maturity levels, you'll need to shift from having a team of Maestros and Makers to having a team of Marketers and Modellers. You'll also see shifts within the individual quadrants towards more senior skill sets around automation, optimization, and operations as opposed to ongoing execution of one-off campaigns.

SHIFTS IN OPERATING MODEL

Your main operating model for marketing will also change. At the Hack level, since the most senior resources will be occupied with establishing your platforms, your operating model for marketing will mostly use trial and error. Every campaign will basically be made from scratch as a small or large project depending on the scope of the campaign. Your team will slowly discover which insights and content work best. Paid and owned media teams will operate separately.

At the Pack level, your operating model will gradually change as you split your owned media execution team into a campaign team and a marketing automation team. This is because campaigns can easily swallow up all of your team's time. If you allow that to happen, you'll never attain the incremental benefits of automated marketing that works even when the lights are out in the marketing department. It's perfectly fine to start out with a project mindset, working on making the campaigns more efficient and reusing and automating as much as possible. This way, you will gradually be able to free up senior resources to build marketing automation for every single moment-of-truth insight that you have. The team will continue working with this project-based mindset until the most obvious marketing automation flows have been built.

At the Stack level, your team will come together across channels. Their focus will be on the customer journey – from an omnichannel point of view. Only a few manual campaigns will remain, since most will have been productified into reusable insights and their content implemented in your martech stack. Each product will represent a specific part of the customer journey. These products will be subject to optimization through an agile operating model with inspiration from agile product development projects.

Once again, we can look at how Netflix works with an agile operating model to continually improve its customer journey (see *Figure 32*). Netflix has an agile and circular operating model where hypotheses are continually tested using experiments. The results are then measured and conclusions are drawn to decide whether there has been an improvement that should become a permanent part of the product. The company then starts a new experiment using either an updated version of the previous hypothesis or a totally new one.[7]

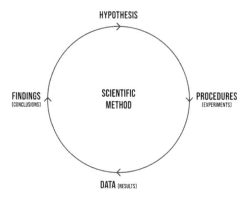

Figure 32. Netflix's agile operating model for continuously improving their product offering, including their marketing and retention communication.

During one of the expert committee meetings conducted during the research process for this book, Martin Bjerg, former Head of CRM at the Danish telecommunications company YouSee, recounted how YouSee had switched to an agile way of working within CRM. Initially, the company adopted the agile development methodology quite literally, with daily morning stand-ups where everyone shared their work scope and potential challenges for the day. The team then moved towards a looser adoption where they kept the concepts of 14-day sprints, each constituting one cycle similar to that of Netflix.

SIZE MATTERS

Large organizations can have their own permanent teams covering all four quadrants. However, in the case of Pernille and the Royal Danish Theatre (at the start of this chapter), the size of the operation and organization does not allow them to have a permanent Maker team of web and app developers. Realizing this from the beginning, they chose to outsource these initial implementation projects to agencies. As soon as their platform projects had been completed sufficiently to allow stable operations, they shifted the focus to a more internal team of Marketers.

Small organizations can have trouble affording and recruiting for specialist roles, such as data scientist. And even if this isn't the case, specialists tend to thrive best when working with peers of the same professional background, so they can be hard to retain if they are hired in the first place. In the case of the Royal Danish Theatre, Pernille's team shares a data analyst employee with other departments. Other members of her team solve tasks that aren't at the core of their skill set. They function as so-called T-profiles, meaning they can solve a wide array of tasks to a satisfactory level but also have an area where they can go deep. This is quite normal in small organizations. If new headcount cannot be approved and specialist people (I-profiles) cannot be hired, the existing team members will have to cover multiple roles – at least, if there's no budget for outsourcing this role to an agency.

INSOURCING VS OUTSOURCING

In general, you should consider outsourcing a skill if your need is temporary – either while a specific platform implementation project is going on or until a planned hire can be completed. Also consider outsourcing if you believe the specialist skill will be hard to find or recruit, or you can't find full-time work for that position.

We've seen organizations visualize their team needs in models resembling an old-school equalizer together with their agencies, as in the example shown in *Figure 33*. In this model, each slider represents a role. The size of the slider represents how much this role is needed. The positioning of the slider represents how the need can be covered (internally or through outsourcing). As discussed above, different configurations are desirable across the three maturity levels. In the model below, for instance, the team shifts from having a preponderance of Makers that are primarily outsourced to having a large team of Marketers that are primarily internal.

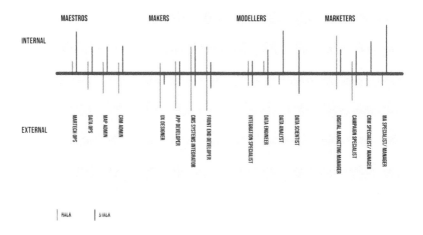

Figure 33. Hack vs Stack – people and skills.

MATURITY LEVELS FOR PEOPLE AND SKILLS

We will conclude this chapter by visualizing the three maturity levels for the Skills and Teams dimension of the Pyramid of Personalization. Pernille's team at the Royal Danish Theatre are clearly on their way from the Pack level to the Stack level.

At the Hack level, the focus is on platforms staffed by a team of Makers and Maestros with significant help from agencies. At the Pack level, the organization matures from executing rather simple, disconnected campaigns to having a mixture of campaigns and marketing automation, each run by a dedicated team. Agencies support the team in key roles that are hard to recruit or retain, or are only needed part time.

The great shift in focus from execution (at the Pack level) to journey (at the Stack level) implies a change towards a more agile and process-oriented operating model with teams working customer-centrically and across channels. The teams and the organization have internal ownership of the process but use agencies occasionally for inspiration or for accelerating traction.

PYRAMID OF PERSONALIZATION- BACK END

ORGANIZATIONAL MATURITY

PEOPLE AND SKILLS

STACK

JOURNEY FOCUS
AGILE OPERATING MODEL
CROSS-FUNCTIONAL TEAMS
INTERNAL DATA ANALYSTS
AGENCY SUPPORT FOR EXTRA PAIRS OF HANDS

PACK

EXECUTION FOCUS
SEPARATE TEAMS BY MARKETING DISCIPLINE
AGENCY SUPPORT ON KEY ROLES

HACK

PLATFORM FOCUS
IN-CHANNEL CAMPAIGN EXECUTION
HEAVY USE OF AGENCIES

CHAPTER 20

MARKETING TECHNOLOGY

'Morten, we need to discuss this!' Amanda said. 'We're risking wasting money and we're potentially sending irrelevant information to our customers Saturday after Saturday.' Amanda was in charge of all marketing automation at Norsk Rikstoto, the Norwegian horse race betting company. Due to outdated technology, every Saturday all customers with an SMS consent received a message promoting that day's V75 horse races regardless of whether they'd already placed a bet or not. This meant that Rikstoto was most likely sending irrelevant communications to many of its customers. This, in turn, meant that customers might begin to think communication from Rikstoto overall held little value for them, so they might not notice communications even when they were relevant.

Morten had been responsible for marketing and ecommerce at Rikstoto for more than 20 years. Around 13 years ago, the team had acquired an early breed of marketing automation platform, which was now clearly nearing the end of its life. Morten asked Amanda to dig further into the case. She found several use cases where Rikstoto was spending more money on communication than necessary, on both owned and paid channels. Furthermore, Morten and his team knew that they weren't personalizing their website for either anonymous or known customers. New legislation making third-party cookies illegal was also coming, and the team needed to ensure that they were compliant and that they didn't lose the first-party data they could and should register and use.

Morten aligned with his internal stakeholders. Lars, the Chief Technology Officer, identified the same issues as Morten and his team, but from another angle. It soon become clear that Rikstoto needed a proper review and sound advice on how to proceed. The company hired a top agency to help with a full review of its martech stack based on its situation and requirements.

With all the tools and channels the team were using, there was clearly an issue with not having a central customer profile that could be kept up to date at all times. It seemed that a lot of the internal processes and solutions related to customer data and communication were fragmented and fragile. The team would need not only a new marketing automation platform but also a whole new way of integrating and aggregating customer data from various sources in real time. On the basis of the agency's report, Morten knew he could get top management on board and start transforming the marketing operations at Rikstoto.

Thinking back to *Chapter 18*, beyond insights and content, the last 'atom' at each level of marketing productization is 'features', and features are found within technology. They might be part of the standard functionality or customized features tailormade for your business. No marketing organization has only one piece of technology. As a result, personalization is done across your **technology stack**. The stack is the set of technology you use when communicating with your customers and prospects. Research from MartechTribe shows that the average stack contains 20 to 40 technology solutions in total.[1] The actual size depends on the company's maturity, as research consistently points out. The more mature the company, the more pieces of technology it is likely to use.

SYSTEMS OF RECORD

Over 20 years, Gartner has developed the PACE layered model, which is a methodology for choosing applications to support business change, differentiation, and innovation.[2] Within this model, the **systems of record** are foundational to any technology stack and removing them is not possible without harming the revenue stream. In addition to systems of record, there are **systems of differentiation** and **systems of innovation**. As new systems become better integrated in a martech stack and their features become used as part of productized marketing, these systems too can qualify as systems of record. In *Figure 34*, the boxes in the two rightmost columns are our addition on top of Gartner's original levels.

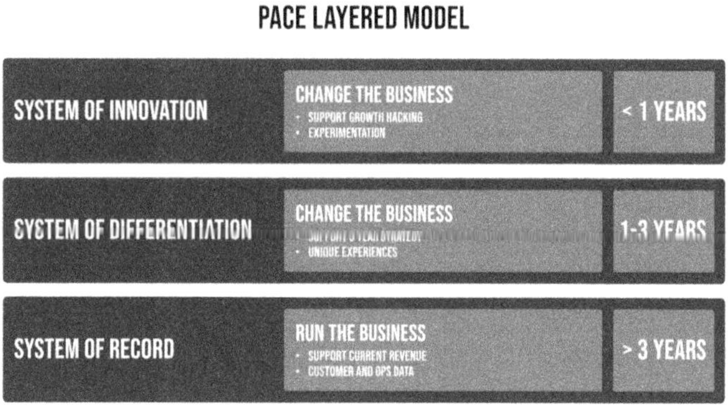

PACE LAYERED MODEL

SYSTEM OF INNOVATION	**CHANGE THE BUSINESS** • SUPPORT GROWTH HACKING • EXPERIMENTATION	< 1 YEARS
SYSTEM OF DIFFERENTIATION	**CHANGE THE BUSINESS** • SUPPORT 3 YEAR STRATEGY • UNIQUE EXPERIENCES	1-3 YEARS
SYSTEM OF RECORD	**RUN THE BUSINESS** • SUPPORT CURRENT REVENUE • CUSTOMER AND OPS DATA	> 3 YEARS

Figure 34. The PACE layered model.

MartechTribe has conducted research into more than 900 martech stacks. Across these stacks, 10,000 vendors showed up frequently. By categorizing these vendors, it was revealed that there are five typical systems of record within martech stacks.

In *Figure 35*, we can see the types of solution that are typically implemented along with the growing maturity levels of martech stacks. Note that the maturity levels in this case are based on the respondents' self-assessed maturity on the Capability Maturity Model Integration (CMMI)[3] scale (from 1 to 5) and, as such, are not directly translatable to our Hack, Pack, and Stack levels.

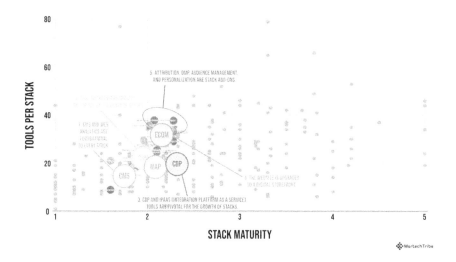

Figure 35. How martech stack maturity correlates with the implementation of systems of record (DMP: data management platform, see the text below for explanations of the additional abbreviations).

The figure reveals a very interesting point, namely the order in which the systems of record are typically implemented into martech stacks as they mature over time. At first, when stacks are relatively small and immature, companies start with a **content management system (CMS)** and soon after add a web analytics solution. Now customers have a place to visit online and traffic can be tracked. Soon after, companies typically also implement a **customer relationship management (CRM)** system. The CRM stores customer profile data centrally. Usually at this stage, companies have also implemented some sort of email service provider (ESP) to send out simple campaign emails. This is not considered a system of record at this maturity level, however.

At the second stage of maturity, companies typically add a **marketing automation platform (MAP)** to replace the ESP. The MAP orchestrates both personalized campaigns and marketing automation towards customers and prospects. At the same stage we see an upgrade of the website to **ecommerce (eCom)**. Often this starts as a static web shop in addition to the website, but it soon grows into an ecommerce portal. The ecommerce portal should be understood in the widest sense: it is not only selling products and services but also supporting customers via a client environment such as a web or mobile app.

There is a fourth system of record on the rise that can be used to manage customer data, the **customer data platform (CDP)**. The aim is not to replace the MAP or the CRM system. It is an addition. Whereas the CRM and the MAP store core customer and lead data (the 'what' of data), the CDP is more focused on making it easy to understand the insights from customer interactions and transactions in real time. Thus, the CDP aims to support the efficient (even real-time) orchestration of insights across execution platforms. This is exactly where Morten and his team from Rikstoto stood in their considerations at the beginning of this chapter. They needed a CDP to enable them to react in real time and comply with responsible gambling policies.

In summary, the five systems of record within marketing are as follows:

1. Content management system (CMS)
2. Customer relationship management (CRM) system
3. Marketing automation platform (MAP)
4. Ecommerce
5. Customer data platform (CDP)

Each of the platforms comes in different flavours or types and caters to different needs. It is your task to know what your company needs. However, as we can see from *Figure 34*, the general tendency across existing martech stacks is that the systems of record will become relevant one by one as the martech stack maturity evolves. Gradually, as your marketing becomes more productified (see *Chapter 18*), more sustainable value creation will be built into each system. Thus, the term 'system of record' will apply to more and more systems over time.

WILL A CUSTOMER CONTENT PLATFORM (CCP) EMERGE?

As we shall see, the central production and management of content (both messages and content feeds) form part of the second glass ceiling mentioned in *Chapter 18*: between the Pack and Stack maturity levels. We see a potential sixth system of record emerging here – the **customer**

content platform (CCP). The purpose of this platform would be to unify the creation and orchestration of messages, offers, and product and other content feeds. In a webinar on likely martech trends in 2023, Scott Brinker and Frans Riemersma forecasted that having one source from which to orchestrate content across channels ('a content layer') will become equally as important as having data available in the same manner ('a data layer').[4] We believe that in the future, AI will play as great a role in crafting content as it does today in calculating insights.

There are several candidates that could fill this technology position in the market – digital asset management (DAM) systems, product information management (PIM) systems, MAPs, or headless CMSs.[5] For non-commerce companies, MAPs, DAM systems, or headless CMSs are in a good position. For commerce companies, PIM systems or commerce systems themselves are positioned well. The CCP could very well be the sixth system of record to emerge as more companies achieve maturity within personalization.

ATOMIZATION AND AGGREGATION

The number of marketing technology providers exceeded 10,000 globally in 2022. However, the number of solutions in stacks has been relatively stable for years at around 20–40.[6] How does this add up?

Over the past ten years, it has often been suggested that there will be a shake-out or consolidation of the supply side of the martech market. But the figures have proven that suggestion wrong, year after year.[7] Research by MartechTribe shows that smaller and younger companies are generally rated better than older and bigger solutions.[8] On the supply side of the martech market, we see a trend that we could call **martech atomization**. Martech atomization can be described as the tendency for there to be an increasing number of small, intuitive tools that do one task extremely well and can be seamlessly integrated into the martech ecosystem.

The same research reveals another trend that takes place on the demand side of the martech market: **martech aggregation**. Martech aggregation can be described as the clustering of key martech capabilities to drive customer experience and value.

GO FOR BEST-OF-INTEGRATION

What does this mean for you as a marketer? It means that your work with campaigns, marketing automation, and inbound platforms is atomizing too. You will be crafting all of your customer experiences using the three key marketing atoms introduced in *Chapter 18* – insights, content, and technology features – just as if they were Lego blocks.

An important element in the martech aggregation trend is what we call **best-of-integration**. Best-of-integration refers to choosing the technology vendors that most easily integrate with the rest of your stack, regardless of whether they are considered independent vendors or belong to a suite of technology from one of the largest vendors.

Whereas the martech market is atomizing, company stacks are aggregating. Thus, integration is key to your ability to cluster features, insights, and content. An increasing number of solutions offer **native integrations** in addition to their **application programming interface (API)**. Both allow for integrating workflows and data between two tools. However, the first is more often plug-and-play and done by marketing (technology) experts, whereas IT involvement is required to develop an API.

In addition to native integrations, there is an entirely new type of technology emerging: **integration Platform as a Service (iPaaS)**. iPaaS is a plug-and-play solution that allows marketers to create any integration they need. The sole purpose of iPaaS is integration between two or more other tools. Many iPaaS solutions have connections with over 1,000 martech solutions.

GROWING YOUR STACK'S MATURITY

As discussed in *Chapter 1*, Gartner describes the adoption of new technology as following a hype cycle.[9] This is shown in *Figure 36*.

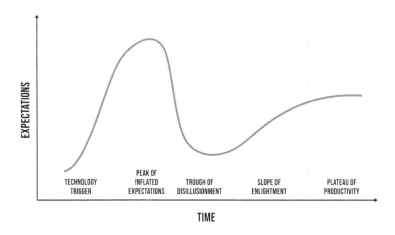

Figure 36. The Gartner hype cycle.

To begin with, expectations are too high and there are many disappointments. The trough of disillusionment is where the glass ceilings are hit. Things are going so well and you are getting results on your channels – surely more of the same will create even better results? Sadly not. This is where most organizations stumble and chief marketing officers change jobs and/or technology. Regardless, during this process you will have found some gems – things that did work really well. That is the foundation for enlightenment and will ultimately lead you on to the plateau of productivity.

When you're designing your martech stack, understanding the hype cycle is a lifesaver. It helps you to see how new technologies are adopted. A key point is that the hype cycle does not just apply to new technologies in the market – it also applies to technologies new to your company, or even to you as an individual.

Along the hype cycle, you will hear different opinions at different stages about the new technology (see *Figure 37*). This will help you to navigate and understand where your company, a team, or an individual is in getting to grips with new technology.

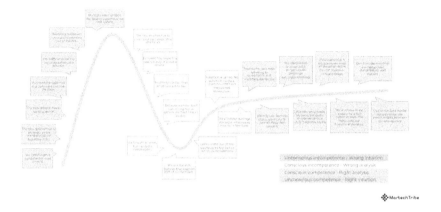

Figure 37. Four stages of technology competence: markets, companies, and individuals all have their own learning curves.

RIGHTSIZING YOUR MARTECH STACK

Let's return to the stack research discussed above. When looking at where the over 900 stacks sit in terms of maturity, we see an interesting correlation with the stack size (i.e. tool count). As *Figure 38* shows, the more mature a stack, the more tools there are. At the least mature level, companies start defining their needs. At the middle level, they have a shared and standardized understanding of their needs. At the top level, they have productized and automated their key customer experiences.

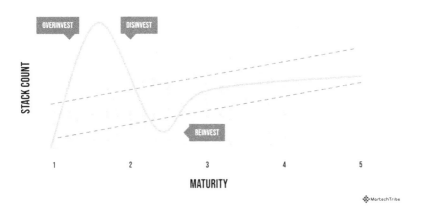

Figure 38. Flattening the martech hype cycle: navigating your team
through the various stages.

By using the maturity model and counting the number of solutions in your stack, you can start rightsizing your stack. The secret is to make sure that you don't buy too many tools at the beginning, putting unrealistic faith in solutions. It should be your goal to find ways to flatten the curve and stay within the dotted lines, which will involve grooming your stack on a regular basis. This will prevent your company from financing an expensive (hyped) learning curve.

USING ATOMIZATION AND AGGREGATION TO RIGHTSIZE YOUR MARTECH ARCHITECTURE

When deciding on a best-of-suite or best-of-breed, it helps to look at the decision-making process from an atomization–aggregation perspective. Your question should not be 'What customer experiences might we need in the future?' Your question should be 'Can we build those customer experiences that will really drive value?' To answer this question, you need to know what exactly drives value for the customer and your company. This is an atomized way of looking at your core needs.

To determine what drives value in this way, you'll need to answer two further questions. Simply put, these are 'How do we make money today?' and 'How do we intend to make money tomorrow?' In other words, what is your current business model, and what is your strategy for the next two or three years? Think about the systems that you cannot switch off without directly harming your current revenue stream. Then define what customer experiences you know will generate future money but are not in place today.

When researching 23 real-life business plans for the Beeckestijn Business School in the Netherlands, Frans Riemersma and his team found that on average, no more than 2.3 features, 4.6 data points (insights), and 5.3 content items were used for each critical phase of the customer journey.[10] As a rule of thumb, it is safe to assume that for every value proposition, you will probably not need more than three to five of each of the marketing atoms (i.e. (technology) features, insights, and content). If you think about it, no specific solution drives value, but a handful of features do. Not all datasets drive insights, but a few key data points do. Not all your content drives conversion, but a handful of evergreen pieces do. It is your task to do your data science homework to find those key items.

MATURITY LEVELS FOR MARKETING TECHNOLOGY

In the below table we've summed up the technology maturity levels for the back end of the Pyramid of Personalization. Morten's team at Rikstoto are clearly on their way from the Pack level to the Stack level due to their need for a CDP and their requirement for centralized and real-time insights on their customers. Their MAP supports central messages to an extent that currently meets their needs.

At the Hack level, the focus of an organization is on implementing a CMS and potentially a CRM platform. Investments should be made following a best-of-integration paradigm to make interoperability as easy as possible.

At the Pack level, the need for replication, automation, and productization of marketing requires the implementation of ecommerce and MAPs. These both produce and need data to operate, and thus require a focus on data integrations to ensure smooth operations.

PYRAMID OF PERSONALIZATION - BACK END
ORGANIZATIONAL MATURITY

TECHNOLOGY

STACK

CUSTOMER CONTENT PLATFORM FULLY INTEGRATED
CUSTOMER DATA PLATFORM FULLY INTEGRATED
STANDARD OPERATING PROCEDURE FOR INTEGRATIONS
MULTIPLE ATOMIZED TOOLS IN STACK
ONGOING STACK TRIMMING AND RIGHTSIZING

PACK

ECOMMERCE FULLY INTEGRATED
MARKETING AUTOMATION PLATFORM FULLY INTEGRATED
DATA INTEGRATIONS SECURED THROUGH DATA OPERATIONS
CLEAR MARTECH ROADMAP GUIDES TECHNOLOGY INVESTMENTS

HACK

PLATFORM PROJECT APPROACH
EMAIL SERVICE PROVIDER IN USE FOR NEWSLETTERS
CRM SYSTEM INTEGRATED FOR ALL B2B
CONTENT MANAGEMENT SYSTEM AND WEB ANALYTICS IMPLEMENTED
INVESTMENTS THROUGH BEST-OF-INTEGRATION PARADIGM

CHAPTER 21
GOVERNANCE

'Has the Clinique email campaign gone out yet?' Iben asked. Peter knew that it had gone out and that Iben had nothing to worry about. He didn't blame her for asking, though. Working at the Danish award-winning beauty and health retailer Matas had been quite a ride and selling campaigns to suppliers hadn't always been as streamlined a process as it was today. Matas was blessed with a very loyal customer club of 1.7 million members and a very high share of transactions attributable to these members. This meant that they were basically sitting on a gold mine of first-party data – first-party data that their suppliers would, well, not literally die for, but at least pay substantial amounts of money to use through supplier campaigns. On that premise, Matas had grown its own retail media, which now contributed quite a lot to the company's bottom line.

It wasn't a given that the Clinique email had gone out. There were usually a lot of candidates for each day's campaigns. The key thing for Matas, though, was always to ensure that its customers had a good experience. So, the team had additional communication flows that weren't selling at all but were full of helpful advice and relevant offers. On top of this, they had to market and sell the products of their suppliers as well as sell their own private-label products. In addition to this were organizational news and notifications. In practice this meant the team constantly had to prioritize customer satisfaction (e.g. net promoter score), supplier obligations, margins on suggested products, and *internal stakeholders. There could easily be five competing messages or campaigns in one day and they couldn't just send everything to everyone. Luckily, they had marketing technology that enabled them to both segment their club members and personalize the content. Tech was rarely the biggest issue – more important was creating the rules for aligning which content went out to whom. It hadn't been easy, but now they had alignment from all stakeholders. Everyone had agreed to the suppression and send-out rules they were now enforcing.*

Peter thought about this for a moment and it dawned on him how many different rules and processes they had to comply with – marketing consents, GDPR compliance, HR policies, IT governance – and to top it all off, the company was also listed on the Nasdaq stock exchange, which came with its own set of requirements. All these governance rules and processes were there for a reason. Some were self-imposed and actually made things easier in the long run. Others were imposed by other departments for the exact same reasons – but seen from their perspective. And then there were the ones determined by law. Not much to do about those – but being an award-winning household brand with so many members and data meant that Matas was scrutinized much more often than the smaller brands.

Governance within marketing and personalization is basically a matter of how you control and manage the use of people, skills, software, content, and data to maximum effect while ensuring legal compliance.

HOW DOES GOVERNANCE APPLY WITHIN MARKETING?

There are three main questions to consider when discussing governance:

- What is governed?
- Who is governing it?
- How is it executed?

Fifty years ago, there was far less governance within marketing. Companies were marketing cigarettes (or even worse drugs) with very few limitations. Today, some industries are hit way harder by legal constraints. The pharma industry perhaps wins the prize for the most regulated industry, but finance is not far behind. In general, governance is applied for a sound reason – even when it feels annoying and bureaucratic.

Within marketing, you'll work with governance originating from legislative requirements, company-wide policies, and internal policies within marketing. It always feels better to adhere to processes and rules that you yourself have imposed to avoid the risk of mistakes that break productivity, but keep in mind that all compliance is there for a reason. And quite often the reason is to help increase productivity, increase employee wellbeing, reduce corruption, or generally make the world a better place.

Governance is typically executed through the definition of and adherence to processes that ensure compliance with the relevant rules or laws. In the case study of Matas that opens this chapter, the main reasons for imposing the suppression and send-out rules are to reduce organizational friction, gain more satisfied customers and suppliers, and ultimately make more money in the long run. But, at the same time, the emphasis on retail media is there because the GDPR (General Data Protection Regulation) does not allow Matas to sell customer data to other parties.

In terms of privacy, this is a good thing for the consumer. And in this case, it's also a good business case for Matas in terms of the quality of its personalization. In Europe, GDPR compliance means that, among other things, companies now have to make it possible for consumers to revoke their data consent and have personal data deleted, or simply gain insight into the data a company has on them. Compliance with this law hasn't exactly driven extra revenue for any business-to-consumer companies, although relatively few consumers now choose to revoke their consent and obtain insights into their customer data. However, the law is definitely a part of making it feel safe and pleasant to live in Europe. Ultimately, it has meant that many companies have far better control of their data and are thus much more ready to do sound and ethically responsible personalization.

Though organizational governance is no new concept, very little has been written about how it affects marketing and thus personalization. Nor has much been written about which kind of governance marketing organizations themselves could benefit from developing and imposing. The following is therefore very much a product of the research process for this book (as described at the start) as well as the experience of the authors.

WHAT IS SUBJECT TO GOVERNANCE WHEN IT COMES TO PERSONALIZATION?

'A lot' is the answer to this question. The following is a non-exhaustive list of governance topics that we've discovered affect personalization in marketing organizations:

- Data processing, privacy regulations, and consent management
- IT
- Procurement processes
- HR policies
- Brand guidelines
- Personalization accountability
- Data operations
- Marketing operating model
- Contact and suppression policies
- Retail media policies
- Martech

The following sections explore these topics in detail, dividing them up into topics imposed by law, topics imposed by other departments, and topics you should consider imposing within your own department.

GOVERNANCE TOPICS IMPOSED BY LAW

Legal matters can differ from country to country or even state to state. If your company is operating across territories, chances are that your company chooses to comply with the most strict legislation among the territories. This means that almost all marketing departments are under-laid with some sort of legally imposed governance.

DATA PROCESSING, PRIVACY REGULATIONS, AND CONSENT MANAGEMENT

All customer data used for personalization is, in practice, personal data. In the European Union, consumers are protected under the GDPR. The CCPA (California Consumer Privacy Act) looks after Californians and Canada has its Anti-Spam Legislation. Similar laws exist in other countries and territories. It's important that you have terms and conditions, secure storage, and documentation, along with processes in place to keep all of this updated.

Compliance is normally the responsibility of a chief data officer or your legal office (or a company lawyer in smaller companies). You will need to have data-processing agreements in place with all subcontractors (including martech suppliers) that are processing your customer data. Keep in mind recent trials within this field, such as Schrems II.[1] The European Court of Justice doesn't look too kindly on the personal data of European citizens ending up in countries that it deems to be less secure, such as the USA or worse.

Complying with data-processing and privacy regulations naturally has consequences for personalization, since everyone involved needs to know and respect these regulations. This is easier, in turn, if appropriate measures are taken in terms of how roles and rights are implemented in the systems in use. This is an important task for the Maestros in your marketing team (see *Chapter 19*).

Managing consents from customers is also a part of ensuring compliance with privacy regulations – and, of course, anti-spam regulations. As a general rule of thumb, and in line with, for example, the GDPR, customers need to actively give their consent before you are allowed to send them anything that isn't related to something they have already bought or a legal hygiene communication (such as a change to terms and conditions or the use of an active subscription). They also need to give their consent for the use of various types of cookie as well as how data is stored and used for personalization (among other things). This is typically described in your terms and conditions. Bear in mind that there is still a lack of clarity in this field – some legal departments won't allow the export of first-party data into paid media ecosystems at all, even if the data is hashed or pseudonymized.

The more transparent your terms and conditions, the more your customers will be consciously aware of what is happening and the more easily you will be able to perform explicit personalization (as discussed in *Chapter 3*). You should make sure to record exactly which terms and conditions or consents each individual has accepted, as these may change over time.

Be aware that there are local differences in how marketing consents have to be given. In Germany, for instance, a so-called double opt-in is currently required for lawful use of marketing permissions.[2] In practice, this means that a customer has to sign up online and then confirm this via an actual received email before the consent is given.

It is the responsibility of marketing to ensure that consents are respected when marketing is sent out or when personalization is performed on a website or an app. Training can and should be implemented to inform and refresh all employees working in these fields. Failure to comply can result in nasty fines. At the time of writing, Meta (Facebook) has just been fined more than $400 million for violating EU privacy rules.[3]

Additionally, failure to address legal issues related to data-processing agreements in a timely manner can greatly delay the acquisition of marketing technology. It's best to involve your legal department or chief data officer sooner rather than later.

The above may sound like a big deal to manage, and indeed it was a large undertaking in many European companies when the GDPR was rolled out. In the case of Matas (at the start of this chapter), the team's impression is that the GDPR no longer takes up much of their attention. It has been adopted seamlessly into their technology and their ways of working.

GOVERNANCE TOPICS IMPOSED BY OTHER DEPARTMENTS

IT GOVERNANCE

IT departments in larger organizations normally have a say when new technology is acquired and implemented. Sceptics say that this is a counter-reaction to Gartner's historic prediction in 2012 that the chief marketing officer (CMO) would be outspending the chief information officer on tech by 2017.[4] In reality, IT has always played a role in defining other departments' technology strategies and which tools (from which vendors) are predominantly used. However, before the GDPR was implemented, it wasn't uncommon for CMOs to go rogue and build their own 'shadow IT' with their trusted agencies and vendors of their own choice. This was perhaps out of impatience at needing to involve IT from the beginning or at having their range of potential vendors limited by a department that didn't necessarily understand marketing practices and what was needed to reach budgets.

Since the advent of the GDPR, it has become increasingly difficult for rogue CMOs to bypass IT departments when acquiring new technology. Ultimately, the purpose of involving IT is, of course, to ensure interoperability and synergies between systems. IT can also help to establish selection criteria and decide organizational ownership of new systems – and of the customer data that is often created from these systems. Rogue CMOs rarely have these areas covered.

Our advice would be to involve IT sooner rather than later when you are looking to acquire new technology. The consequence of not doing so can easily be a substantial delay. It will most likely be IT that will be supplying a lot of the data and integrations you need to run the platforms you are acquiring. You might as well address everything all at once.

PROCUREMENT PROCESSES

Most software salespeople dislike the involvement of procurement departments in the acquisition process for any software tool. The same goes for agency owners, who often (but less frequently) also experience the need to deal with procurement departments. Many marketers dislike it as well.

The main purpose of the procurement department is to avoid the organization spending more money than necessary and to steer clear of potential nepotism. The procurement department will often require a vendor selection process where comparable vendors are evaluated and pitted against each other to create a list of the best two or more vendors that meet the requirements. Then, the price is squeezed and the most optimal solution is chosen from a contractual point of view. It takes time, but generally procurement departments do save organizations money and help to qualify processes and streamline contracts.

Again, our advice would be to involve procurement sooner rather than later when you are looking to acquire new technology. Some organizations, especially in the public sector, have strict spending thresholds over which any purchase has to undergo a structured procurement process.

HR POLICIES

HR – or the more recent synonym 'people and culture' – will generally intersect with marketing less than IT, legal, or procurement. As organizational maturity around personalization increases and reaches the Pack and especially the Stack level, however, HR becomes increasingly important. HR generally has the responsibility to ensure that people are treated fairly and that the organization's employees reach and retain a high level of skill. This often means implementing procedures for crafting role descriptions as well as designing compensation schemes and incentives that are aligned across the board. Naturally you have to follow suit.

When you become ready to split (and potentially expand) your marketing team into separate campaign and marketing automation teams, you should partner up with HR to make sure you agree on new role descriptions and corresponding packages for compensation and benefits. The same goes for when you are ready to transition your team to a journey-based approach.

BRAND GUIDELINES

Admittedly, this one is perhaps within the boundaries of marketing's remit. Brand guidelines are often defined within marketing – but in large organizations, the brand team can be a silo of its own. It's not necessarily a marketing technologist's highest priority to ensure 100% compliance with a corporate visual identity.

However, if you are doing large-scale implementations of design-heavy assets – such as a website, an app, or an extensive email marketing automation set-up – then you should check whether any new brand guidelines are in progress and align with them. It's a waste of time and money having to reimplement a new design minutes after an implementation is considered 'done'.

GOVERNANCE TOPICS YOU SHOULD CONSIDER IMPOSING

Not all governance is about complying with the law or helping other departments to reach their goals. Some governance is needed internally within marketing if you want to succeed with personalization.

PERSONALIZATION ACCOUNTABILITY

It is important to secure realistic expectations around personalization. To achieve this, we advise any marketing leader to develop principles for measuring and reporting the success of personalization and how much it contributes in terms of additional engagement, sales, customer lifetime value, and customer satisfaction. Not all chief executives pose the right questions to their CMO. So, in order to ensure that you aren't asked the wrong questions, it's better to start the conversation and deliver your suggestions on key performance indicators (KPIs) and a proper reporting format. As we discussed in *Chapter 14*, make sure to use control groups to determine the relative effects of communicating with personalization versus generically.

Especially when you're first starting out with personalization, it's important to align expectations. If you have little scale in your customer database and have yet to implement core tools (e.g. a content management system and a marketing automation platform), it will take quite some time to deliver real monetary results from personalization on owned media. Additionally, when you are transitioning to more automated communication at the Pack level, it is important to consider the timing dimension. Specifically, marketing automation must be measured using a whole other time span than traditional campaigns.

The shift to the top level (Stack) also often implies a change in the metrics you should measure. Instead of focusing on sales or conversions, you can start monitoring more customer-journey-centric and thus more omnichannel metrics, such as customer lifetime value and net promoter score. Make sure to prepare your senior peers for this shift.

As we discussed in *Chapter 17*, it's actually hard to do any advertising without some degree of personalization. So, measuring an additional uplift coming from personalization seems a bit off. We suggest you instead measure and report what additional uplift you are getting from audiences built on your first-party data as well as the money you save by excluding selected audiences, as we described at the end of *Chapter 11*.

Make sure you align and share progress with both senior management and your team members so that everyone knows how you are doing. Having proof of value will make it a lot easier for you to defend the licence cost of software, your advertising budget, and the headcount you need. Remember to factor in the labour costs and the spend on consultants. Otherwise, you will have a fake number for your return on investment.

DATA OPERATIONS

Once you start using multiple martech applications that rely on data, you will realize that data isn't just data. This is where policies for data operations come in. Policies for data formats, consistent and meaningful field naming, and table names and structures all make a big difference when you have people working across systems. The format, structure, and processes that IT prefers to deliver this data most likely won't be what you'd optimally like to help your marketers execute more easily. Remember that IT don't have responsibility for the execution or an understanding of what it takes, so be prepared to stand your ground on what you need.

Data operations (data ops) is a function that belongs in the Maestro quadrant of the skills we discussed in *Chapter 19*. It becomes really important once you reach the Pack level of organizational maturity for personalization.

MARKETING OPERATING MODEL

Only what is described can be repeated – especially by someone else. And once it's automated it's also much easier to improve. Make sure you describe processes and checklists for marketing and personalization tasks. These will help you improve and automate and thus move closer to real marketing productization at the Stack level.

CONTACT AND SUPPRESSION POLICIES

As we saw in the example from Matas at the beginning of this chapter, in larger organizations customers can easily be bombarded with communications across channels from various well-meaning departments. And if this is already the case when you are 'only' sending out campaigns, how can you then justify adding more communication flows in the form of marketing automation?

Developing and implementing a contact and suppression framework will help you to execute more efficiently. It will ensure that your customers don't receive more communication than you see fit and that the communication they get will be what you expect them to find most relevant.

A simple rule could be that each highly engaged customer can, at most, receive one campaign per day but that they will not get this if they have already received a piece of automated communication within the past five hours. Another rule could be to always ensure a balance between inspirational and helpful emails. For instance, after a purchase has been made, you could suppress inspirational emails and instead send instructional and informative emails for a week or so related to the product's category, brand, or type. You will naturally have to uncover the right rules for your business. Bear in mind, too, that the more you include internal stakeholders from other departments, the less you will have to explain yourself over and over again.

RETAIL MEDIA POLICIES

In direct relation to your contact and suppression policy, you should include category and product managers in discussions on how you plan to prioritize campaigns for suppliers. What are the priorities in terms of target groups and your own planned campaigns? And how about sponsored products in your product feeds? Which placements do sponsored products get in a category? And what if you have a higher margin on your private-label products? What is shown first then? It's better to enter retail media with open eyes and have these discussions up front.

MARTECH GOVERNANCE

Just like we covered in the section on IT governance, introducing martech-specific governance will make sense once you have ownership of a considerable martech stack. Make sure that you manage contracts, applications, usage, data flows, and policies across the board. In this way, 'marketing operations' will be in charge of marketing platforms. This is clearly another task for a person within the Maestro role.

MATURITY LEVELS FOR GOVERNANCE

Addressing the above points in how you approach governance will greatly improve your chances of succeeding at and excelling with marketing and personalization.

We are not saying that you should abandon them once you move up to the next level. However, you will likely change how they are implemented according to the descriptions above and your current level.

We will conclude this chapter by visualizing the three maturity levels for the Governance dimension of the Pyramid of Personalization. Peter's team at Matas, which we touched upon going into this chapter, have clearly progressed to the top Stack level with their implementation of communication suppression and retail media policies.

At the bottom Hack level, the focus is on getting the marketing systems of record in place. This process is heavily influenced by legal, procurement, and IT policies. In addition, we suggest imposing a personalization accountability process already at this stage, as this will be instrumental in getting approval for further investments all along the way to the top of the pyramid.

At the middle Pack level, there is an increasing need for clean and efficient data integrations (data operations) fuelling the new operating model that HR has helped the marketing teams progress into.

PYRAMID OF PERSONALIZATION - BACK END

ORGANIZATIONAL MATURITY

GOVERNANCE

STACK

MARTECH GOVERNANCE
CONTACT AND SUPPRESSION POLICIES
RETAIL MEDIA POLICIES

PACK

HR POLICIES
MARKETING OPERATING MODEL
DATA OPERATIONS

HACK

PERSONALIZATION ACCOUNTABILITY
BRAND GUIDELINES
IT GOVERNANCE
PROCUREMENT PROCESSES
MARKETING LEGISLATION COMPLIANCE

CHAPTER 22
ACHIEVING ORGANIZATIONAL MATURITY FOR PERSONALIZATION

We've now seen how people and skills, software, and governance play equal parts in constituting the maturity levels. You need a team with the right skills to implement and operate the software you acquire. The team should grow from a team of builders across your own organization (and potentially supporting agencies) towards a predominantly internal team of executors covering both campaigns and marketing automation. Ultimately, the teams will join in a journey-focused agile operating model where your marketing becomes productified.

When it comes to software, no personalization happens at scale without software. However, there's a logical order for incorporating the various types of platform.

Finally, governance evolves alongside your team, skills, and software maturity. To begin with, you liaise with procurement, IT, and legal. Then data operations become key along with HR. Eventually your own internalization of martech governance becomes necessary to rightsize your stack based on a sound martech strategy.

THE GLASS CEILINGS AND HOW TO BREAK THEM

Just knowing the levels of the back end of the Pyramid of Personalization doesn't necessarily help you to move from one level to the next. In this short chapter, we share what we see as the actions you need to take in order to break through the otherwise invisible glass ceilings preventing you from rising to the next level and becoming a true star within personalization. Our suggestions are summarized in *Figure 39*.

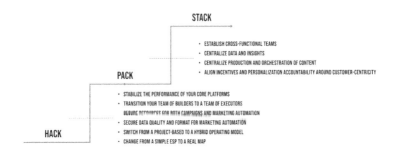

Figure 39. Breaking through the glass ceilings.

BREAKING THE GLASS CEILING BETWEEN THE HACK AND PACK LEVELS

First, let's have a look at what could potentially keep you from breaking through the glass ceiling between the first two levels: Hack and Pack.

STABILIZE THE PERFORMANCE OF YOUR CORE PLATFORMS

If you still haven't stabilized the performance of your core website, your ecommerce platform, and potentially your app, then you will have a hard time directing customers anywhere to make them convert and become more valuable. Fix your platforms in terms of technical performance (to secure uptime) and search engine optimization, and in terms of working with conversion rate optimization to strengthen conversions in the core customer experience.

TRANSITION YOUR TEAM OF BUILDERS TO A TEAM OF EXECUTORS (MAKERS TO MARKETERS)

At the Hack level, your focus should be on your core platforms. This requires a team of builders, namely the Makers. Don't expect this same team to excel at executing personalized communication in both campaigns and marketing automation. It's one thing to build the car and another to drive it. Align with HR to smooth this transition.

SECURE RESOURCES FOR BOTH CAMPAIGNS AND MARKETING AUTOMATION

Marketing automation is not an exercise in cost savings. Don't expect the same junior marketers who have built your one-off email campaigns for years to suddenly become skilled enough to do marketing automation while having enough time to be making campaigns in tandem. You want to be operating two separate teams to ensure overwork on campaigns doesn't get in the way of progress on marketing automation. Get your personalization accountability working for you to help you secure the proper headcount.

SECURE DATA QUALITY AND FORMAT FOR MARKETING AUTOMATION

IT takes care of customer data from an accounting and GDPR point of view, but not an execution point of view. That's where you need to get involved and take responsibility for data quality and especially format. If possible, anchor this task with a specialized Maestro who carries the title of data operations manager or similar.

SWITCH FROM A PROJECT-BASED TO A HYBRID OPERATING MODEL

The part of your team that works with marketing automation should not follow the same operating model as the people who work with campaigns. It makes sense to establish your marketing automation platform through an implementation project. However, once this is done, the team should switch to an agile operating model with an iterative process focus: hypothesis, experiment, conclusion, productification.

CHANGE FROM A SIMPLE ESP TO A REAL MAP

Don't judge a fish by its ability to climb trees. And don't expect a simple email service provider to work for marketing automation. Specialist tasks require specialist tools. An email marketing platform will never enable automated personalized experiences across channels. Make the change to support your new organization.

BREAKING THE GLASS CEILING BETWEEN THE PACK AND STACK LEVELS

Moving from the efficiency level of Pack to Stack also involves breaking a glass ceiling.

ESTABLISH CROSS-FUNCTIONAL TEAMS

Moving from the split team focus of campaigns and marketing automation to journey-centric teams is by no means an easy task. Again, HR needs to be involved. In smaller organizations, some resources will need to be shared across teams. The important things are to align the teams around the customer journeys and make sure their metrics follow suit.

CENTRALIZE DATA AND INSIGHTS

As your marketing teams now work across channels with customers at the heart, they all need to draw on the same insights. The logic for determining segments and moments of truth thus needs to be centralized. This also makes it possible to apply AI to a greater extent to help you determine messages in line with the next best experience (see *Chapter 11*).

CENTRALIZE PRODUCTION AND ORCHESTRATION OF CONTENT

Building content within channels makes it very inefficient to produce – and, more importantly, to manage and orchestrate. Centralizing both messages and content feeds and matching them with insights before any channels are applied is not an easy task. New systems need to be bought and potentially customized to make this happen.

REALIGN YOUR INCENTIVES AND PERSONALIZATION ACCOUNTABILITY AROUND CUSTOMER-CENTRICITY

With a new operating model, team structure, and focus, you need to align incentives around your new customer metrics accordingly. This will also mean a change in how you manage accountability for personalization. Liaise with HR to make this come alive for the team. Make your peers in the organization aware of the shift and about how reporting and results will be communicated from now on. If you keep measuring the old metrics, you'll get different results from the ones you're after.

CHAPTER 23
CONCLUSION

Personalizing by using the first name of customers in direct mail and emails suddenly seems so basic . And indeed it is. We've now covered serious ground in coming to understand personalization at a deeper level.

Our initial goal with this book was to define personalization in a way that was broad enough for practitioners to use across marketing disciplines. The definition paved the way for the Bowtie of Personalization as a model for understanding the concept and the parts that make it up. We then looked at how these parts come together and create value in the three marketing disciplines of campaigns, marketing automation, and inbound platforms (see *Figure 40*).

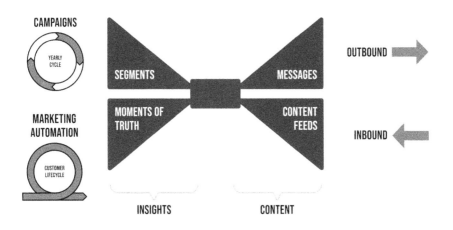

Figure 40. The complete Bowtie of Personalization.

But what could and should you build, and in what order? We next introduced three levels of maturity for the scope of personalization across the three disciplines in the form of the Pyramid of Personalization – or at least the front end of it.

Pausing for a bit, we looked at the prerequisites for making personalization the right choice of communication tactic. What needs to be in place before you can double down on it?

Assuming these prerequisites were in place, we then moved on to cover how you can support personalization from an organizational point of view and make it efficient at each step. How is the front end of the pyramid supported by the back end? In other words, we gave our answer to the question of how you can work with people and skills, software, and governance to make personalization across channels become truly game-changing. *Figure 41* summarizes the front and back ends of the pyramid.

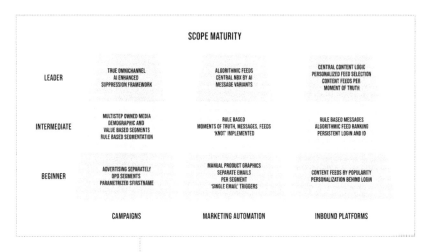

Figure 41. The complete Pyramid of Personalization.

We hope you've enjoyed the ride and found the concepts and the models in this book useful. Our goal is for you to be able to embark and excel on the journey towards a truly value-creating personalized customer experience for customers and your company alike.

ABOUT THE AUTHORS

Rasmus Houlind, the main author of this book, is a well-known writer, speaker, and consultant in the Nordics. After ten years of consulting within digital marketing and marketing automation, in 2015 he published his first marketing book (in Danish), *Hvis det handler om mig, så køber jeg!* (*If It's About Me, I'll Buy!*). In 2019 he followed up with the omnichannel marketing bestseller *Make It All About Me* from LID Publishing. Since then, he has evangelized omnichannel marketing and marketing automation from his position as Chief Experience Officer with the Nordic martech company Agillic. He has worked with organizations such as Red Cross, PureGym DK, Tivoli, Matas, Bolia, SPORTMASTER, Imerco, Varner-Gruppen, Andel Energi, and Telge Energi.

Frans Riemersma has spent the past two decades researching martech capabilities, stacks, and vendors together with over 250 global members of his so-called MartechTribe (www.martechtribe.com). The resulting database contains no fewer than 10,000 vendors, 1,000 real-life stacks, and 4,000 martech-wide requirements. This all forms the basis for publishing vendor landscapes, benchmarking and selecting software, and designing martech stacks for companies such as HP, Adidas, Audi, BASF, Unilever, Philips, ABN AMRO, Pandora, Standard Bank, Swift, and Volvo. This background puts Frans in a unique position to explain how organizational maturity within personalization looks from the martech and governance angles. Consequently, Frans contributed considerably to *Part IV*.

Arild Horsberg has been in the personalization business for more than 30 years and is considered the 'grand old man' in this arena by many Norwegians. In 1992, Arild started Mailbox, which later became Bas Kommunikasjon – today the largest agency within marketing automation, analytics, and personalization in Norway. In 1997 he founded Dialogkonferansen, which has grown to become the leading conference on customer relationship management (CRM), personalization, and customer experience in the Nordics.

Mattias Andersson is one of the co-founders of the multiple-award-winning martech consulting company Miltton Insights. In addition, Mattias is a frequently engaged speaker within customer relationship management (CRM) and data-driven marketing. He also participates in various Swedish and international marketing award jury groups. Before co-founding Miltton Insights, he was, among other roles, Head of CRM Analytics at Scandinavian Airlines, CRM and Customer Club Manager at Twilfit, and Head of Analytics at the mobile operator 3. He contributed to the book *30 Advice from 30 Greatest Professionals in CRM and Customer Service in the World* (2017).

ACKNOWLEDGEMENTS

The authors would like to thank the following people for their invaluable contribution to making this project come alive.

EXPERT PANELISTS

Alexander Elling, Samsung Electronics Nordic, Senior CRM Specialist

Camilla Østerberg Madsen, Yousee, Director of CRM and Customer Engagement

Charlene Walkoff, Active Brands, Director of Loyalty and Customer Engagement

Charlotte Guldmand, Danske Bank, Head of Digital UI and Design Systems

Dorte Karlsson, Web2Media, Senior Advisor and Business Developer

Emil Hagan, Eika Group, Marketing Director

Gitte Blemings, Danish Church Aid, CRM Manager

Hans-Kristian Bjerregaard, Founder of Clerk.io

Hilde Haustreis, Bas Kommunikasjon, Marketing Automation Specialist

Janneke Tranås Marino, Gjensidige, SVP of Consumer Market and CX

Jared Lekkas, Mentimeter, Director of Product Marketing

Jonathan Behr Mattsson, Flyttsmart, Head of Marketing & CRM

Jørgen Sando, Varner, CRM and Customer Insights Manager

Karsten Juul, Impact Extend, Director of Technology

Kim Jong-Andersen, WDPX, CCO and Partner

Kim Skjoldborg, Dwarf, Partner and Head of Business Development

Kirsten Petersen, PureGym Denmark, CRM Manager

Lisa Björnskär, 3 Sverige, Head of Customer Growth & Loyalty

Lotte Bork Ferraro, Velliv, Head of Marketing and Customer Experience

Mads Vangkilde, EssenceMediacom Denmark, Strategy Lead

Malin Nygren, Musti Group, Chief Customer Officer

Marianne Stjernvall, Queen of CRO/bubbi.ai, Founder/Advisor and Partner

Martin Bjerg, Danske Spil, Marketing Director

Mats Rönne, OffPist Management, Senior Advisor

Mikkel Pilemand, Nemlig.com, Chief Commercial Officer

Morten BW Tønnessen, Norsk Rikstoto, Marketing Director

Niklas Gustavsson, Mindwile, Founding Partner

Pepe Larsson, Smicker, Founder, Head of Strategy & Innovation

Per Lobedanz Witthøfft, JourneyWise, CEO

Peter Boris Kreilgaard, COOP.dk, Chief Commercial Officer

Peter Hestbæk, Matas, Head of Digital Sales and Marketing

Peter Hvidberg, Imerco, Director of Omni-commerce and Service

Peter Schlegel, Responsive, CEO

Petra ter Laak, Coolstuff,Chief Marketing Officer

Petter Andersson, Engagement Factory, Sales Director Nordics

Rasmus Bidstrup, Dwarf, Marketing Automation Tech Lead

Sara Mundt-Petersen, Coop Sverige, Business Director E-Com and Customer Meetings

Sarah Hoof, mySafety Försäkringar, Chief Commercial Officer

Sofie Okstad, Gents.com, Marknadschef

Stefan Kirkedal, Matas, Head of Customer Insights, Loyalty and Matas Media

Sven Johansson, Synsam, Head of CRM

Søren Mohr, Nestlé, Nordic Media and Digital Manager

Therese Aagaard, Bertel O. Steen, Customer Lifecycle Manager

Thomas Lindvig, eBizConsult, Founder

Thomas Obelitz Høgsbro-Rode, Impact Extend, Senior Partner and co-CEO

Tomas Gorrissen, NexusAmbition, Client Service Director

William Sillemann, Miinto.com, Head of Digital Marketing

Åsne Graver, Gjensidige, Director of Marketing & CRM

NARRATIVE PROTAGONISTS (IN ORDER OF APPEARANCE)

Kirsten Petersen, PureGym Denmark, Head of Member Experience

François-Yves Caya, Desjardins Group, Director of Marketing and Customer Strategy

Jesper Holm-Pedersen, SPORTMASTER, Loyalty and Customer Engagement Manager

Marie Goddard, Financial Times, Director of Customer Relationship Management

Pier Luigi Spagna, Warner Bros, VP of EMEA Retention and Engagement

Morten Tønnesen, Norsk Rikstoto, Marketing Director

Pernille Rasch, Danish Royal Theatre, Marketing Director

Peter Anders Franck, Matas, Head of Customer Insights, CRM and Email Marketing

ADDITIONAL INTERVIEWEES AND CONTRIBUTORS

Alex Christensen, Pandora, Automation and Performance Manager, Global Email Marketing

Alexandra May, Movable Ink, Associate Director, Corporate Communications

Andreas Månsson, Ericsson, GF M&C Data and CRM Director

Casper Heiselberg, Tivoli, Head of Digital

Chris Gibbins, Creative CX, Chief Experience Officer

David Mannheim, Made with Intent, Founder and Author

Emil Björnskär, Miltton Insights, Senior Consultant and Head of Martech and Partnerships

Emre Gürsoy, Agillic, CEO

Gianfranco Cuzziol, Natura and Co, Group CRM and Personalisation Head

Gibson Biddle, Former Netflix/Chegg VP Product, Speaker, Teacher and Workshop Host

Hans-Peter Bech, TBK Consult, Author and Consultant

Jacob Holst Mouritzen, Strategy Consultant

Jesper Reismann, ex Hugo Boss, Senior Vice President Omnichannel

Joe Zappa, Sharp Pen Media, Founder and Principal

Jon Lombardo, LinkedIn, Global Head of Research

Jordi van Rijn, eMailMonday, independent e-mail and Marketing Automation Consultatnt

Kasper Holst, Impact, CEO

Kaviraj Khurana, Pomelo Fashion, Product Manager

Ken Leaver, End Game Tech Consulting, Product and Strategy Consultant

Klaus Silberbauer, ManyOne, Global Partner

Mads Jefsen, F.C. Copenhagen, Marketing Director

Maike Haberkorn, MoEngage, Customer Centricity and Digital Marketing Expert

Malthe Cederborg, Miinto.com, CMO

Margareta Willman, Head of Society, Eidsiva

Marlene Maarbjerg, Kop & Kande, Head of Omnichannel and Marketing

Martin Jonassen, Podimo, Chief Data Officer

Martin Wammen, Valtech, VP Martech Consultancy Services

Maxie Schmidt, Forrester Research, Vice President, Principal Analyst

Nils Hafner, Hochschule Luzern, Speaker, Blogger and Professor

Per Dyring Dahlberg, Storytel, Global Head of CRM Sales and Operations

Peter Loell, Omnicom Media Group Denmark, Technology Therapist

Rusty Warner, Forrester Research, Vice President, Principal Analyst

Sofia Svensson, Red Cross Sweden, Head of Individual Giving

Tekila Harley Nobile, USI Università della Svitzera Italiana, Post-doctoral Researcher and Lecturer

MORAL SUPPORT

In addition to the above-mentioned people, Rasmus Houlind would like to furthermore express his deep-felt gratitude to his wife Line Groot and their kids Esther, Nora and Kornelius Houlind for their patience with an occasionally overworked and mentally absent father. Thank you! You are the love of my life!

NOTES

INTRODUCTION

1. Nat Ross, 'A History of Direct Marketing' (unpublished paper, 1992).
2. Shobhana Chandra, Sanjeev Verma, Weng Marc Lim, Satish Kumar, and Naveen Donthu, 'Personalization in Personalized Marketing: Trends and Ways Forward', *Psychology & Marketing* 39, no. 8 (2022): 1529–1562.
3. David Mannheim, The Personalization Paradox (London: Brown Dog Books, 2023).
4. See, for instance, Gibson Biddle, 'A Brief History of Netflix Personalization' (Medium), 1 June 2021, gibsonbiddle.medium.com/a-brief-history-of-netflix-personalization-1f2debf010a1; and Larry Hardesty, 'The History of Amazon's Recommendation Algorithm' (Amazon Science), 22 November 2019, www.amazon.science/the-history-of-amazons-recommendation-algorithm.
5. E.g. Peter Weinberg and Jon Lombardo, 'Forget Personalisation, It's Impossible and It Doesn't Work' (*Marketing Week*), last modified 6 May 2022, www.marketingweek.com/peter-weinberg-jon-lombardo-personalisation-impersonalisation.
6. See the chapter 'Acknowledgements' in the back of this book for the full list of contributors.

1. THE HYPE OF PERSONALIZATION

1. Don Peppers and Martha Rogers, *The One to One Future* (London: Piatkus, 1993).
2. Rasmus Houlind and Colin Shearer, *Make It All About Me: Leveraging Omnichannel and AI for Marketing Success* (London: LID Publishing, 2019).
3. Nidhi Arora, Wei Wei Liu, Kelsey Robinson, Eli Stein, Daniel Ensslen, Lars Fiedler, and Gustavo Schüler, 'The Value of Getting Personalization Right—or Wrong—Is Multiplying' (McKinsey & Company), last modified 12 November 2021, www.mckinsey.com/capabilities/growth-marketing-and-sales/our-insights/the-value-of-getting-personalization-right-or-wrong-is-multiplying.
4. Nidhi Arora, Wei Wei Liu, Kelsey Robinson, Eli Stein, Daniel Ensslen, Lars Fiedler, and Gustavo Schüler, 'The Value of Getting Personalization Right—or Wrong—Is Multiplying' (McKinsey & Company), last modified 12 November 2021, www.mckinsey.com/capabilities/growth-marketing-and-sales/our-insights/the-value-of-getting-personalization-right-or-wrong-is-multiplying.
5. *Drive Customer-Centric Business Growth With Omnichannel Marketing Automation Maturity*, a commissioned study conducted by Forrester Consulting on behalf of Agillic, May 2022, agillic.com/forrester-study.
6. 'Client Story: Miinto & Agillic' (video), agillic.com/client-stories-miinto/.
7. Renewing Matas, Q1 2020/21 Update, 24 August 2020, Investor.Matas.dk, https://s23.q4cdn.com/244975451/files/doc_presentations/2020/08/Q1_20-21_Roadshow-Presentation.pdf
8. 'The Martech Landscape' (Chief Martec), accessed 10 March 2023, chiefmartec.com/wp-content/uploads/2022/05/martech-landscapes-2011-2022_1456px.jpg.

9. Scott Brinker, 'Marketing Technology Landscape 2022: Search 9,932 Solutions on Martechmap.com' (Chief Martec), last modified 3 May 2022, chiefmartec.com/2022/05/marketing-technology-landscape-2022-search-9932-solutions-on-martechmap-com.

10. MartechTribe.com – get detailed URL

11. 'Gartner Hype Cycle' (Gartner), accessed 18 January 2023, www.gartner.co.uk/en/methodologies/gartner-hype-cycle.

12. Dave Chaffey, 'Latest Gartner Hype Cycles for Digital Marketing: 2009–2022' (Smart Insights), last modified 2 October 2022, www.smartinsights.com/managing-digital-marketing/marketing-innovation/technology-for-innovation-in-marketing.

13. This graphic in figure 3 is made on the background of the various hype cycles published from 2014 until 2022 by Gartner, Inc. www.gartner.com/en/research/methodologies/gartner-hype-cycle

2. WHAT IS THE PROBLEM WITH PERSONALIZATION?

1. 'Gartner Predicts 80% of Marketers Will Abandon Personalization Efforts by 2025' (press release, Gartner), last modified 2 December 2019, www.gartner.com/en/newsroom/press-releases/2019-12-02-gartner-predicts-80--of-marketers-will-abandon-person.

2. Peter Weinberg and Jon Lombardo, 'Forget Personalisation, It's Impossible and It Doesn't Work' (*Marketing Week*), last modified 6 May 2022, www.marketingweek.com/peter-weinberg-jon-lombardo-personalisation-impersonalisation.

3. DEFINING PERSONALIZATION

1. Tekila Harley Nobile and Nadzeya Kalbaska, 'An Exploration of Personalization in Digital Communication: Insights in Fashion', in *HCI in Business, Government and Organizations*, eds Fiona F.-H. Nah and Keng Siau (Cham: Springer, 2020): 456–473.

2. Steffen W. Schilke, Udo Bleimann, Steven M. Furnell, and Andrew D. Phippen, 'Multi-Dimensional- Personalisation for Location and Interest-Based Recommendation', *Internet Research* 14, no. 5 (2004): 379–385.

3. Kashmir Hill, 'How Target Figured Out a Teen Girl Was Pregnant Before Her Father Did' (Forbes), last modified 16 February 2012, www.forbes.com/sites/kashmirhill/2012/02/16/how-target-figured-out-a-teen-girl-was-pregnant-before-her-father-did.

4. 'Personalization' (Gartner), accessed 18 January 2023, www.gartner.com/en/marketing/glossary/personalization.

5. Tekila Harley Nobile and Lorenzo Cantoni, 'Personalization and Customization in Fashion: Searching for a Definition', *Journal of Fashion Marketing and Management* (2022), doi.org/10.1108/JFMM-09-2021-0224.

6. Gibson Biddle, 'Netflix's Customer Obsession'(Dialogkonferansen), Gothenburg, Sweden, 19 September 2022.

7. Gibson Biddle, '#1 The DHM Model' (Medium), last modified 12 July 2019, gibsonbiddle.medium.com/2-the-dhm-model-6ea5dfd80792.

4. WHY DOES PERSONALIZATION WORK?

1. Tekila Harley Nobile and Nadzeya Kalbaska, 'An Exploration of Personalization in Digital Communication: Insights in Fashion', in *HCI in Business, Government and Organizations*, eds Fiona F.-H. Nah and Keng Siau (Cham: Springer, 2020): 456–473.

2. Ville Salonen and Heikki Karjaluoto, 'About Time: A Motivation-Based Complementary Framework for Temporal Dynamics in Web Personalization', *Journal of Systems and Information Technology* 21, no. 2 (2019): 236–254.
3. Vladas Griskevicius and Douglas T. Kenrick, 'Fundamental Motives: How Evolutionary Needs Influence Consumer Behavior', *Journal of Consumer Psychology* 23, no. 3 (2013): 371–386.
4. Ville Salonen and Heikki Karjaluoto, 'About Time: A Motivation-Based Complementary Framework for Temporal Dynamics in Web Personalization', *Journal of Systems and Information Technology* 21, no. 2 (2019): 236–254.
5. *State of the Connected Customer* (Salesforce, 2022), www.salesforce.com/resources/research-reports/state-of-the-connected-customer.
6. Nidhi Arora, Wei Wei Liu, Kelsey Robinson, Eli Stein, Daniel Ensslen, Lars Fiedler, and Gustavo Schüler, 'The Value of Getting Personalization Right—or Wrong—Is Multiplying' (McKinsey & Company), last modified 12 November 2021, www.mckinsey.com/capabilities/growth-marketing-and-sales/our-insights/the-value-of-getting-personalization-right-or-wrong-is-multiplying.
7. 'Amazon Alexa Echo Recorded Conversation and then Sent to Contact' (CBS News), last modified 25 May 2018, www.youtube.com/watch?v=S7ta4CfXu1Y.

5. MARKETING WITHOUT PERSONALIZATION

1. Nidhi Arora, Wei Wei Liu, Kelsey Robinson, Eli Stein, Daniel Ensslen, Lars Fiedler, and Gustavo Schüler, 'The Value of Getting Personalization Right—or Wrong—Is Multiplying' (McKinsey & Company), last modified 12 November 2021, www.mckinsey.com/capabilities/growth-marketing-and-sales/our-insights/the-value-of-getting-personalization-right-or-wrong-is-multiplying.

6. THE BOWTIE OF PERSONALIZATION

1. How millennials actually want brands to engage with them, NAPCO Research commissioned by Bluecore Marketing, July 2016, www.bluecore.com/blog/do-millennials-use-email/.
2. Michael J. Naples, *Effective Frequency: The Relationship between Frequency and Advertising Effectiveness* (New York: Association of National Advertisers, 1979).

8. CONTENT, PART 1: MESSAGES

1. Martin Jonassen, personal meeting with Rasmus Houlind, Copenhagen, Denmark, July 2018.
2. 'Brand Translation Troubles: When a Dictionary Is Simply Not Enough' (Language Reach), last modified 6 February 2015, www.languagereach.com/brand-translation-troubles-dictionary-simply-enough.
3. 'Hello Moto' commercial, Motorola (YouTube), accessed 10 March 2023, www.youtube.com/watch?v=iOkgLQdyQOs.
4. 'NFHS-5: Indians are getting fatter - and it's a big problem' (BBC News), accessed 10 March 2023, www.bbc.co.uk/news/world-asia-india-61558119.
5. 'Identifying and Prioritising Category Entry Points: What are CEPs and why are they important' (Ehrenberg-Bass), accessed 10 March 2023, www.marketingscience.info/

research-services/identifying-and-prioritising-category-entry-points/.
6. Maxie Schmidt, 'What Customers Value' (CX EMEA), London, UK, 22 June 2022.
7. Chris Keating, 'Secrets of direct mail 1: the extraordinary findings of professor Siegfried Vögele' (SOFII), accessed 10 March 2023, sofii.org/article/secrets-of-direct-mail-1-profes sor-siegfried-vogele.
8. 'Average time people spend reading brand emails from 2011 to 2021' (Statista), accessed 10 March 2023, www.statista.com/statistics/1273288/time-spent-brand-emails/.

9. PERSONALIZATION IN CAMPAIGNS

1. Rasmus Houlind and Colin Shearer, *Make It All About Me: Leveraging Omnichannel and AI for Marketing Success* (London: LID Publishing, 2019).
2. Personal conversation between Jesper Holm Pedersen (SPORTMASTER) and Rasmus Houlind, Copenhagen, Denmark, 17 November 2022.
3. Dorte Karlsson, 'Storyhouse Egmont' (Digital Copenhagen), Copenhagen, Denmark, November 2019.
4. Benjamin Broomfield, 'How Warner Bros. Discovery is Scaling Email Personalization' (ClickZ), last modified 5 December 2022, www.clickz.com/how-warner-bros-discovery-is-scaling-email-personalization/267799/.
5. 'Geomatic', geomatic.dk/en/ and 'Mosaic' (Experian), www.experian.co.uk/business/plat forms/mosaic, both accessed 10 March 2023.
6. Terence Kawaja, 'Retailers Are Launching Media Networks Because' (LinkedIn post), last modified October 2022, www.linkedin.com/posts/terencekawaja_retailers-are-launching-media-networks-because-activity-6986707832444231681-LpHo.

10. INSIGHTS, PART 2: MOMENTS OF TRUTH

1. Gibson Biddle, 'Netflix's Customer Obsession'(Dialogkonferansen), Gothenburg, Sweden, 19 September 2022.
2. See, for instance, 'Upplysning.se', www.upplysning.se or 'Numberplade.net', www.num merplade.net, both accessed 10 March 2023.
3. Jim Lecinski, *Winning the Zero Moment of Truth* (Google, 2011), www.thinkwithgoogle.com/marketing-strategies/automation/2011-winning-zmot-ebook.
4. Sridhar Ramaswamy, 'How Micro-Moments Are Changing the Rules' (Think with Google), last modified April 2015, www.thinkwithgoogle.com/_qs/documents/56/how-micromoments-are-changing-rules.pdf.
5. Rasmus Houlind and Colin Shearer, *Make It All About Me: Leveraging Omnichannel and AI for Marketing Success* (London: LID Publishing, 2019).

11. PERSONALIZATION IN MARKETING AUTOMATION

1. Rasmus Houlind and Colin Shearer, *Make It All About Me: Leveraging Omnichannel and AI for Marketing Success* (London: LID Publishing, 2019).
2. Jørgen Sando and Erica Munthe-Kaas, 'The Power of Data & Loyalty' (Dialogkonfer-ansen), Gothenburg, Sweden, 20 September 2022.
3. Malthe Cederborg, Miinto client story video, agillic.com/client-stories-miinto/.
4. 'Aarstiderne', accessed 10 March 2023, www.aarstiderne.com.

5. Dorte Karlsson, 'Storyhouse Egmont' (Digital Copenhagen), Copenhagen, Denmark, November 2019.
6. Lisa Björnskär, Expert Committee Meeting, Stockholm, Sweden, 13 October 2022.
7. Marie Goddard, 'Fact Checking Personalisation' (webinar), London, United Kingdom, 10 February 2021, agillic.com/videos/.
8. Mads Jefsen, Agillic Client Story, agillic.com/client-story-f-c-kobenhavn-agillic/.
9. Margareta Willman, Agillic Summit, Copenhagen, Denmark, 28 May 2018.
10. Dorte Karlsson, 'Storyhouse Egmont' (Digital Copenhagen), Copenhagen, Denmark, November 2019.
11. Brandon Purcell, 'The Future of Customer Insights Will Power Next Best Experiences' (Forrester Research), last modified 12 February 2021, www.forrester.com/report/Come-Together-Right-Now-To-Deliver-The-Next-Best-Experience/RES143255.
12. Frida Wahlberg, 'From Donation to Automation' (Customer Loyalty Conference), Stockholm, Sweden, 30 September 2020.

12. CONTENT, PART 2: CONTENT FEEDS

1. Mounia Lalmas, 'Spotify: Personalising the Listening Experience' (Alan Turing Institute), last modified 16 December 2019, www.youtube.com/watch?v=IX8ZwVReQMs.
2. Martin Jonassen, Comment on article by Rasmus Houlind, 'Do people always have to notice personalization?', LinkedIn, November 2022, www.linkedin.com/pulse/do-people-always-have-notice-personalization-rasmus-houlind/.
3. Personal conversation between Stefan Kirkedal (Matas) and Rasmus Houlind, Copenhagen, Denmark, 17 March 2022.
4. Ian MacKenzie et al., 'How Retailers Can Keep Up with Consumers' (McKinsey), 1 October 2013, www.mckinsey.com/industries/retail/our-insights/how-retailers-can-keep-up-with-consumers.
5. John Bohannon, 'Is Facebook Keeping You in a Political Bubble?' (Science.org), 7 May 2015, www.science.org/content/article/facebook-keeping-you-political-bubble.
6. Mounia Lalmas, 'Spotify: Personalising the Listening Experience' (Alan Turing Institute), last modified 16 December 2019, www.youtube.com/watch?v=IX8ZwVReQMs, see especially from 27:56.

13. PERSONALIZATION ON INBOUND PLATFORMS

1. Paloma Truong, 'Fact Checking Hyper Personalisation' (Madfest Webinar), London, United Kingdom, 10 February 2021, agillic.com/videos/.
2. Marianne Stjernvall, Expert Committee Meeting, Stockholm, Sweden, 13 October 2022.

14. TYING IT ALL UP IN THE BOWTIE OF PERSONALIZATION

1. See also the model The Omnichannel Hexagon in Rasmus Houlind and Colin Shearer, *Make It All About Me: Leveraging Omnichannel and AI for Marketing Success* (London: LID Publishing, 2019).
2. 'A/B test sample size calculator' (Optimizely), accessed 10 March 2023, www.optimizely.com/sample-size-calculator/.
3. Gibson Biddle, 'A Brief History of Netflix Personalization' (Medium), last modified 1 June 2021, gibsonbiddle.medium.com/a-brief-history-of-netflix-personalization-

1f2debf010a1.
4. David Mannheim, The Personalisation Paradox (London: Brown Dog Books, 2023).

15. THE BASIC FOUNDATIONS FOR PERSONALIZATION

1. 'What Is Brand Trust and Why Is It So Important?' (Qualtrics), accessed 18 January 2023, www.qualtrics.com/uk/experience-management/brand/brand-trust.
2. Fatemeh Khatibloo, Q&A: What Marketers Need To Know About Zero-Party Data (Forrester Research), 10 October 2018, www.forrester.com/report/QA-What-Marketers-Need-To-Know-About-ZeroParty-Data/RES145095.

16. DATA AND PERSONALIZATION

1. See Figure 3 of F. E. Below, Martin Uribelarrea, Matías L. Ruffo, and Stephen P. Moore, 'Triple-Stacks, Genetics and Biotechnology in Improving Nitrogen Use of Corn' (North Central Extension-Industry Soil Fertility Conference, Des Moines, IA, USA, 2007), www.researchgate.net/figure/The-grain-yield-response-of-corn-to-fertilizer-N-rate-and-the-maximum-return-to-N-MRTN_fig3_268186767.
2. 'Gamification Builds a Triangle Win for Kop & Kande', Case study by Playable.com, www.playable.com/cases/kop-kande/.
3. Peter Boris Kreilgaard, 'Are Retailers the New Publishers? Perhaps' (Programmatic Update), Copenhagen, Denmark, 11 November 2022.

17. CONVERSION RATE OPTIMIZATION AND PERSONALIZATION

1. See, for instance, Christine Campbell, 'Will Google kill third-party cookies' (TechTarget), 22 March 2022, www.techtarget.com/searchcustomerexperience/tip/Will-Google-kill-third-party-cookies; and 'Apple block on third party cookies will change digital media forever' (Verdict), 23 June 2021, www.verdict.co.uk/apple-halts-third-party-cookies/.

18. MODELS OF ORGANIZATIONAL MATURITY IN PERSONALIZATION

1. Rasmus Houlind and Colin Shearer, Make It All About Me: Leveraging Omnichannel and AI for Marketing Success (London: LID Publishing, 2019).
2. Drive Customer-Centric Business Growth With Omnichannel Marketing Automation Maturity, a commissioned study conducted by Forrester Consulting on behalf of Agillic, May 2022, agillic.com/forrester-study.
3. Frans Riemersma, 'Successful Marketing Teams Productize Their Marketing' (LinkedIn post), last modified November 2022, www.linkedin.com/posts/fransriemersma_anticonlx-martech-digitalmarketing-activity-6991291129841254400-cvQa.

19. PEOPLE AND SKILLS FOR PERSONALIZATION

1. *Drive Customer-Centric Business Growth With Omnichannel Marketing Automation Maturity*, a commissioned study conducted by Forrester Consulting on behalf of Agillic, May 2022, agillic.com/forrester-study.
2. Stefan Kirkedal, *The State of European Omnichannel Marketing Automation*, 14 September 2022, agillic.com/forrester-study/.
3. Scott Brinker, *Hacking Marketing* (Hoboken, NJ: Wiley Blackwell, 2016).
4. Scott Brinker and Laura McLellan, 'The Rise of the Chief Marketing Technologist', *Harvard Business Review* (July–August 2014), accessed 18 January 2023, hbr.org/2014/07/the-rise-of-the-chief-marketing-technologist.
5. Scott Brinker, 'The Many Splendid Varieties of Marketing Technologists in 2020: Martech Roles and Archetypes' (Chief Martec), last modified 5 January 2020, chiefmartec.com/2020/01/marketing-technologists-martech-roles-archetypes.
6. Scott Brinker, 'The Many Splendid Varieties of Marketing Technologists in 2020: Martech Roles and Archetypes' (Chief Martec), last modified 5 January 2020, chiefmartec.com/2020/01/marketing-technologists-martech-roles-archetypes.
7. Gibson Biddle, 'Netflix's Customer Obsession'(Dialogkonferansen), Gothenburg, Sweden, 19 September 2022.

20. MARKETING TECHNOLOGY

1. Frans Riemersma and Scott Brinker, 'Martech 2023 The Really Big Picture', 6 December 2022, slide 104, www.martechmap.com/download.
2. 'The Need for Speed: Gartner's Pace Layered Architecture' (Codit), last modified 9 April 2020, www.codit.eu/blog/gartners-pace-layered-architecture.
3. Stephen Watts, 'CMMI: An Introduction to Capability Maturity Model Integration' (BMC), last modified 19 February 2020, www.bmc.com/blogs/cmmi-capability-maturity-model-integration.
4. Scott Brinker, 'A Whirlwind Tour of the New Martech Map, Major Martech Trends for 2023, and How to Manage It All in the Year Ahead' (Chief Martec), last modified 7 December 2022, chiefmartec.com/2022/12/a-whirlwind-tour-of-the-new-martech-map-major-martech-trends-for-2023-and-how-to-manage-it-all-in-the-year-ahead.
5. A headless CMS is a CMS without the layout part. Content is stored in a 'pure' form and the styling is applied in the presentation layer.
6. Frans Riemersma and Scott Brinker, *Martech for 2023 The Really Big Picture*, 6 December 2022, slide 104, www.martechmap.com/download.
7. Scott Brinker and Frans Riemersma, *The State of Martech 2022* (Martech United, 2022), slide 8, www.martechmap.com/download.
8. Scott Brinker and Frans Riemersma, *Martech for 2023: The (Really) Big Picture* (Chief Martec, 2022), www.chiefmartec.com/wp-content/uploads/2022/12/martech-for-2023.pdf.
9. 'Gartner Hype Cycle' (Gartner), accessed 18 January 2023, www.gartner.co.uk/en/methodologies/gartner-hype-cycle.
10. Frans Riemersma, LinkedIn, 16 February 2022, www.linkedin.com/posts/fransriemersma_martechtribe-beeckestijn-business-school-activity-7031881800054394881-yIe7.

21. GOVERNANCE

1. 'The CJEU Judgment in the *Schrems II* Case' (European Parliament), last modified September 2020, www.europarl.europa.eu/RegData/etudes/ATAG/2020/652073/EPRS_ATA(2020)652073_EN.pdf.
2. See, for instance, 'Germany: Revised DSK guidance on direct marketing' (DataGuidance), May 2022, www.dataguidance.com/opinion/germany-revised-dsk-guidance-direct-marketing.
3. Ryan Browne, 'Meta Fined over $400 Million by Top EU Regulator for Forcing Users to Accept Targeted Ads' (CNBC), last modified 4 January 2023, www.cnbc.com/2023/01/04/meta-fined-more-than-400-million-in-ireland-over-eu-privacy-breaches.html.
4. Scott Brinker, 'Gartner: 72% Have a "Chief Marketing Technologist" Today' (Chief Martec), last modified 12 September 2012, chiefmartec.com/2012/09/gartner-72-have-a-chief-marketing-technologist-today. Sadly, the original webinar from Gartner.com is no longer available.

Printed in the USA
CPSIA information can be obtained
at www.ICGtesting.com
LVHW062037190923
758702LV00056B/680